Church in a Blues Bar

*Rethinking Evangelism
in a Post-Christian Culture*

ii

Church in a Blues Bar

Rethinking Evangelism in a Post-Christian Culture

Allan W. Dayhoff, Jr., D. Min.

Evangelize Today

2020

Second Printing: March 2015

ISBN 978-1-716-47082-0

Evangelize Today Ministries, LLC
PO Box 7239
Fairfax Station, VA 22039
evangelizetoday@gmail.com

www.evangelizetoday.com

Additional copies available at the following retailers: Amazon.com, Lulu.com, and our website. For other ordering information, contact the USPS address or email listed above.

Song lyrics:
Rights reserved by Emily Morrison and Robbin Moses Kapsalis

Contents

Forward

I was hesitant and a little nervous when I was asked to consider writing a forward for Al's book *Church in A Blues Bar*. What could my still-unfolding journey add to what Al is already saying in the book?

But then I thought..."I guess that's exactly the point". Al's passion and love for people outside our church walls has completely changed my outlook on ministry. Perhaps it will change yours as well.

This new journey of mine into the "wild" outside the church began with the growing realization that perhaps I was not really cut out to be a church planter. I had been laboring in the suburbs of Atlanta with little fruit to show for my efforts. Despite the fact that I had attended a Bible College, a three-year seminary M-Div program, and pastored for 22 years, I knew in the inner recesses of my soul that there was something fake, and I was desperately afraid of being "outed". Although I had always loved evangelism and eagerly participated in the sharing of the Gospel to those outside the Christian community, I truly did not understand why non-Christians didn't jump at my carefully worded explanations and presentations and my plea for them to turn to Jesus. Did these people not understand how much time and money had been spent for me to become an "expert" on faith? Why wouldn't they just *listen* to me?

My frustration grew to the point where I was contemplating leaving the ministry altogether. And in the middle of that disillusionment, God began to graciously nudge me in a new direction. In June of 2016 I received an invitation to a church-planting conference. I went with one simple, desperate plea: "God, help me become a better church planter, or I'm done."

At the conference, I heard Al Dayhoff say things like:

-The Christian community needs to shift from "listening to *reply*" to "listening to *hear*".

-The unbeliever seldom responds to confrontational evangelism. The reality is that non- Christians already have a preconceived notion of what you are going to tell them. They simply want to experience whether or not you really do believe it, and whether you truly care about them.

-The turnstile of evangelism does not pivot on apologetics any longer, but on the common experience of suffering. We must learn to sit with people in the dust.

-The non-Christian world wants to be pastored first, listened to and cared for, and only then will they be open to truth. As we are patient with them, they will tell us when they are ready to hear the Gospel.

As I listened to Al, my passion for evangelism came alive again. Al listened to me, gently counseled me, taught me, celebrated with me, and even grabbed my hand and walked with me into some new situations where I would have never envisioned a fruitful ministry.

My ministry continues to unfold in amazing, grace-filled ways. The way I approach people, and the kinds of people I approach, has forever changed. It's a journey that is changing *me*, as well as the people around me.

My hope is that in the pages ahead, *your* journey is just beginning.

Scott Bull
Grace Community Church
Buford, GA

Preface

Something primordial has changed in our time, world, and culture as it relates to the church and to building faith-bridges to the faith-skeptical. But something else has stayed the same in the timeless truths of the Gospel; a time-tested invitation that can be accessed by the common man — and by the very common man. Jesus said, "Behold I stand at the door and knock." How and where is He knocking?

I invite you to take a risk with me, to ponder the thoughts we share together, to embrace, question, or reject these words. I hope you will give them honest mindshare —test them in the field as well as in the church.

I have spent my life serving in the church, and I believe the core truths of the Christian faith are as real and true today as ever. But we seem to have lost our stride with evangelism, with sharing our faith, and with knowing just where and how the unchurched think, hunt, suffer, or hide.

Dance studios talk about "dancing in the wild." That does not mean wild dancing — it means taking what you have practiced in the dance studio and trying it out on a regular dance floor, maybe in some restaurant or bar with regular people. Some of the thoughts in this book take the opposite path: the ideas sprang up from being out in the world — "in the wild" — and then I had the wild idea to bring them back to the comfortable studio of the church. My heart is for you to love the studio, but also to take your own adventure into the wild, allowing listening to create hearing.

Is the Age of the Church over for Western culture? Or, for a new generation of seekers, has it maybe just begun?

As a church planter in the 1990s, my dream was to grow a new church fellowship to the point of having our own building. If we build it, they will come! Creating a place for everyone, both current members and newcomers, to call home was our goal. I prayed for this well-designed building to let our parishioners use their ministry gifts, a place to develop a loving ethos to grow through Christ. At last, we opened the doors of our 5 million dollar campus, and our building was indeed full.

But "full" was not really full. Our church was full of folks who had transferred from the struggling churches all around us. But who else should we be welcoming? What happened to "Knowing Jesus and making Him known?"

The dream changed now. The pathway God had laid before me disappeared into a fog and I became lost and numb, fighting an internal battle with anger and cynicism. I prayed over and over again, "God, do something — I'm dying here."

And now new doors opened, as the old path disappeared for good. I became a nomad once again, not voluntarily, and I found a new group of other lost nomads. I think of them as my "Blues People." At first, they were just people who, like me, enjoy blues music. As I got to know some of them, I prayed for them, and it changed me. My new discoveries brought fire back into my soul for the ministry.

We need to ask ourselves a question: How far away from us is the closest non-Christian life? The non-Christian used to be a neighbor, a friend, and a possible sympathizer to the Christian walk. Things have changed. Sympathy is hard to find. The non-Christians around us are as distant as if they spoke a foreign language, a language completely alien to those within the church. But they may be closer to thinking about the eternal Gospel questions than we could imagine. Maybe what we need is a new "starting place." Maybe it takes a new kind of adventurer — researcher, missionary — to find a shared language, to hear and understand them.

If the fish are not coming to us, we must go to them. How will we do that?

Chapter 1

Listening in a Blues Bar

Poor me
I can't stop my heart from crying
Poor me, oooh
These tears gotta mind of their own....
Poor me
I'm drowning in a sea of tears and shame
My heart, my heart will never be the same
Poor me me me
I can't fake another day
You know, I know, love don't live this way.

Robbin Moses Kapsalis
Vintage #18

I was driving home in October 2012, on the familiar — but also emotional — trip from my church, six miles away. Things were not well in my head and my heart, and my soul was the traffic cop trying to make sense of the congestion. Tired questions took up too much room inside of me. I heard myself asking, "Does anyone know what it's like to carry a parish around in your head all the time?" My brain felt like a *Nascar* race on TV, engines roaring around the same old track. Whew: at least I had six days before I had to preach again, but it felt like just three.

A sign on the right side of the road caught my attention, a sign for a Sunday night blues jam at a local bar. The button on my radio is set to the blues channel, right next to the one for BBC news. My blues, my truck and dog, sitting by a river with a rare cigar: my secret pleasures that always helped me find and calm my noisy core. People sometimes laugh at blues music, maybe because it cracks open our secret thoughts and exposes the backroom narratives of our lives.

I sure wanted to go into that blues bar on my way home from church — but could I? Could I actually enter that dark den that I had been shaped to be afraid of?

For three weeks I ignored that sign. But finally, one Sunday, I told Deb that I was gonna be out for the evening. I knew she had plenty to do, getting ready for the art classes she taught at a Christian high school. She said, "Great, need dinner?" I said no, I would have roots and sprouts and flax seeds for dinner (our code for McDonald's drive-through).

Why couldn't I tell my wife I was going to a blues bar? Not because she would have disapproved. I just didn't want to crack open my tired, angry, limping flow of thoughts.

Wardrobe selection: blend in with the crowd that would likely show up at a blues bar. Jeans, baseball cap, tee shirt — basic *preacher* camouflage.

After a nervous drive, I parked and walked into a dark room: spooky lighting, musicians up front, and about 30+ people in even darker seats. The smell of beer, leather, and liquor hit me right away. The range of folks sitting there hit me second: men and women, almost all ages, various shades of skin. But it was the fear of being found out . . . as a pastor . . . that hit me hardest.

I sat in the back, feeling very out of place and surprisingly at home at the same time. The floor could barely be seen, and the table was sticky. The waitress called me "honey pie" and asked for my drink order. I said, tea with lemon. "Really, hon?"

This was not a great start, and I hoped for no more questions. I felt like an imposter, sitting with a group of people who warmly greeted one another with real and lingering hugs.

Darnit, for weeks afterward, that waitress had a pitcher of tea ready for me each time I walked in. Yes, I had become a Sunday regular. The place began to be familiar, with remnants of the Saturday night crowd lingering in the barroom (and especially in the bathroom. Oh, the bathroom. Do you wash your hands and use the paper towel to open the door?) People ages 40 to 80 years occupied the seats and the

2

stage: bikers and homeowners and yuppies and at least one "preacher-in-hiding."

And why on earth *was* I hiding here?? After all, I was living out my calling of building a God-glorifying church building. No longer would our congregation be nomads, taking shifts in various school cafeterias. We had started a church 20 years ago, and finally, three years ago, began worshipping in our own "built from scratch" church building. It was a gorgeous building and a great accomplishment; amazing that our young men and women could pull off such a feat. It was the building that mattered, right? You could touch it, walk inside, and feel that you had a church home.

But my church had a pastor who was, let's be honest, pretty terrible at administrative tasks. Often my feet felt like they were in cement that had not yet hardened; I could move them, but only with great determination. Who was in charge of what, anyway? Well, many of the responsibilities were mine. The mortgage became my nightmare. It had to be paid every month! Didn't the bankers understand that we were a nonprofit church, just trying to do good things?

Each Sunday, after the service, I stood at the door to the parking lot to shake the hands of my dear congregants. These were people who lived the blues — in their marriages, health crises, job demands. They dealt with insomnia and family struggles. This was where I felt God's pleasure, pastoring alongside people's hurts. But now that we had our building, I became stuck in daily conversations about the morning's offering, about typos in the church bulletin, about the thermostat setting, about who was assigned for nursery duty that morning. And whose job was this, whose job was that, *whose job was it??*

Something happened, the fourth month I went to my blues bar. The singer and the lead guitar player were singing a song by Stevie Ray Vaughan, *The Sky is Crying*.

"The sky is cryin', can't you see the tears roll down the street..."

Something happened in me. Something got cracked open and got exposed. The message of the song, the word "baby," the singer feeling his music with his fingertips and words. Something caught me by surprise. I felt like crying, and it had been a long time coming. I did it in a quiet, manlike, preacher-in-hiding kind of way. The waitress came over at that exact moment to ask if she could bring more tea, and darnit, she caught me. My guard was down. I was completely vulnerable, completely human.

Body language started speaking all around me. People were connecting with the singer — and not in a happy, "gonna party like it's 1999" kind of way, but quietly. There was a connection between the musicians and the audience of people, people who would probably never talk to each other in sunlight hours. I felt a rocking motion in the music, like an old lady with a new baby, like an autistic child seeking to find his center, like people who needed to cry but had nowhere to go and no one to give them the space for their sorrows.

This is what a lot of blues music is about: how the weight of the human experience is just too much sometimes. "My baby left me" seems to weave through most blues music. But "baby" could be my girlfriend, my wife, my health, my miscarried baby, my dead father who I never said "sorry" to, my waistline, my dog who got run over. Suffering and blues: the common ground for the biker, the yuppie, the waitress, and one hiding pastor. In the blues bar, "I'm sorry, man" is how the men spoke to one another, a hand on a shoulder. The women talked and sometimes cried with the other women. "Forsaken" is the cry; someone to listen is the hidden desire; and *being heard* is the start of redemption.

And people started dancing. I have to tell you that I love to dance. I have great memories of swing dancing in high school, at proms and in the one dance contest my girlfriend and I won because we could put the crazy in swing. And when I've traveled in Africa over the last 24 years, I found that the all-out dancing was the key to connecting later, during the interactive sermon.

But this dancing in the blues bar was different. It was adult, bluesy, a less-is-more kind of movement. The connection between partners was a kind of moving conversation. The musicians, the audience, and the dancers were all grooving to the same beat and the same message: "Yeah, my baby left me." It wasn't a drunken, bawdy, bragging, quick-pick-up kind of environment. It was a philosophy of life that we had all come to know and share, just a band of broken travelers. I began to discover a unique tribe called "blues people". The music, the lyrics, and the company provided some kind of real comfort, like telling someone what hurts and the other person listens and believes you. For me, the pastor, this was a new kind of listening.

4

And maybe that's what the haunting message really was: listen for when your hurt is spoken in a song.

In a confused way, I looked forward to my weekly blues adventure. When I left preaching each Sunday morning, the sign along the road was waiting there to remind me of my appointment later that night. Deb asked me about the blues bar and what it was like inside. I gave her vague answers, I don't know why. I guess I didn't want to admit I was excited about going there. Sunday morning was my calling, my official responsibility . . . and it wasn't much fun anymore. Sunday night had become my recreation, my freedom from responsibility.

It also became a fascinating laboratory where faith could meet real life. For years I had walked on Christian carpet, talked Christian talk to Christians, did Christian handshakes and drank Christian coffee. I had moved farther and farther away from the 83 percent of Americans who are not connected to a church family — drifted away from my first love, as the young, naive church "planter" who actually believed in evangelism. Maybe blues-bar lingo wasn't Christian talk, but it spoke directly to me.

And more: this new adventure had the drumbeat of danger in the background, a thumping that was always in my ears in those days, that I would argue with or try to ignore. I knew I was in danger of losing the war to keep the church going. The mortgage was crushing, the numbers of people dwindling, the conflicts becoming more acrid. Often I just wanted to run away from it all. Was the blues bar really a mask for my failed struggle? Was I taking refuge in this somewhat pretentious pastime in order to make a "meaningful" exit from the church? I was afraid to connect those dots. I wondered if there was too much to lose.

I had been coming to the blues bar every week for four months, sitting in my self-assigned seat, breathing in the conversations around me, making gentle eye contact and doing a few fist bumps with some other people on this weekly blues cruise. I had in fact made the long journey from five tables back to three tables back from the stage. One evening, when the musicians were taking a break, one woman turned to me and asked a basic but frightening question. "What do you do?" she asked bluntly. My mind started spinning and saying, "Was this really happening? This was my refuge, I was off the clock." And the truth was, my baby was not doing very well. My hesitation was, um, awkward, drawing more attention.

The waitress happened to buzz by at that moment. "I think he's a priest," she announced. My internal voice shouted, "Darnit, where did that come from? Had I even spoken to these people?" Well, of course I had. I am a preacher who talks to anyone, maybe not always so subtle about getting into a stranger's hidden story. My camouflage was clearly not working. But the group took the remark sarcastically.

"Did you hear the one about the priest who went into a blues bar?" I was preparing a jokey answer when another woman scrutinized my face and said, "You are, aren't you!" (By the way, a blues bar has only one word for a religious guy, a "priest.") The woman was watching me steadily. The waitress seemed delighted to have caught me sitting in my oh-so-blended duck blind, waiting for unsuspecting birds to land nearby. But when I looked around and saw their faces, I could see that the group was mortified, shading into anger. I felt their shame and hurt.

"Why are you here?" someone challenged me.

"Are we your project?" another said, with an edge of hostility. Even in panic I could visualize the news story: "Preacher gets butt kicked in local blues bar."

The group quieted when the musicians came back on. Things seemed to get back to normal — the new normal. Some people would not speak to me for several weeks, as if I was radioactive. You see, at the bar I had a ringside seat, a peek at the score: who's sleeping with who, who was behind on child support, who needed a place to stay, who was sick of their 6am to 8pm routine, all the crude jokes. People felt betrayed.

But I kept coming back. The place that acted as their refuge from life became mine too. But now something shifted. Each week, someone would ask me to pray for them. They wanted a prayer for their children, or about the court case with the ex, or the unpaid taxes. Someone's child had been screaming on the phone, in hurt or in rage. The health issues brought a special desperation: motorcycle accidents, cancer, and therapist appointments to pay for. And there were "white collar" prayer requests, about downsizing, resumes, and attorney fees.

I was a bit ashamed of my own attitude. I didn't want to be the pastor. I craved being one of the guys; I wanted emotional filling, not draining. This might be a new adventure, but I wasn't sure I wanted in. Selfishly, I wanted to be left alone. I felt an awkward tension, sitting in the supposed "den of sin" while feeling the pleasure — and the pressure — of God's work in and around me.

For my blues friends (as I thought of them) my presence created another kind of tension. They liked me - I could tell. But their distaste for religion kept them cautious, cagey. They would pour out their confidences in a slow, "less is more" kind of tempo, in the hope that someone might possibly be listening. After all, their blues "priest" might have an in with the Guy upstairs. Hidden from view, of course, was the preacher who was also seeking the Guy upstairs.

I had been hanging at the bar for six months, and by now I was the semi-official blues bar preacher. Every week, it seemed, I would be called to the back of the bar to pray with someone who was crying. My presence would often trigger anger: "F*** God and F*** the church!" I was trespassing on their turf, no longer safely ensconced in an elevated pulpit. The anger went deep, going back decades even into their father's story. Anger was often followed by tears revealing feelings they thought were hidden and under control. Strangely, I felt at home here, praying with them, listening to them, never showing shock or disgust at their blaspheming. And each week when I walked in I received lingering hugs and fist bumps from people I had come to know and love.

So, naturally, I asked the blues organizer if we could host a session at my church. "You nuts?" he said. "I'm serious," I assured him, "and we can pay the musicians." A blues player being paid was the magic wand. They came to the church on a Sunday afternoon, seemingly scared that they would be struck by lightning. Yes, about 40 church people came and the blues group of 40 came too. Both groups were suspicious, and a bit wary of each other. Low-cut blouses, cigarette breath, logo boots...my blues buddies weren't exactly church-going types. It was too loud, and the group didn't seem to sync with our church building. It was a risk, an experiment, and some in my congregation took it on with good humor and a great attitude. But despite my good intentions, it simply didn't feel right.

When I came home I asked Deb if I could invite some friends over for a Christmas party. Deb said, "Okayyyy," wondering what was coming at her, what would happen in our front yard and to our reputation. I explained, "Some friends from the blues bar are looking for a Christmas party." Ok, I was stretching the truth. I just wanted to invite them over, maybe to make up for crashing their Sunday blues jam, maybe so I could be one of them, maybe because my church was going downhill. I didn't know why, but at least it would be a fun adventure.

And it was. Fifty people came to our not-so-big house. It was packed, sort of like a popular Friday night happy hour. I even found a Christmas blues "station" on Pandora to play in the background. These were not the church people I spoke to every Sunday morning. But I was beginning to feel at home with my new buds, real people who were willing to give me a chance to pastor. Some of them seemed amazed that this "priest" actually lived in a house, had children and a wife and a dog. Some had a cautious look, almost not blinking in order to stay vigilant and not let the cuss words flow like DC traffic. I saw looks being exchanged, which I interpreted as, "When's the sermon coming?" "What's the catch?" and "I need a smoke, man."

I called for attention to offer a prayer, and everyone bowed their heads. I said thanks for the food, and for each soul in the room, and I asked for help and encouragement for each person at whatever struggle they faced, and then I gave thanks for Jesus at Christmas. When I said Amen, many others whispered "Amen" too.

I didn't know where this was all going. Something new was bubbling inside me — and it was about time, too. Back when Deb and I got married, we moved to Northern Virginia with our two passions, art (hers) and evangelism (mine). As with everyone, we soon got caught up in "doing life": buying a house, fixing it often; managing cars and attending plays and our kids' soccer practices. All wonderful things that make waking up in the morning a joy. But at the same time, I had strayed from my passion. I had moved from evangelism to church maintenance. Deb was able to stay focused on her craft, developing art curriculum, taking art trips to NYC and Europe, earning her masters at the Corcoran Gallery.

And now, where was I? I was now pastoring a group of church transfers, people who were at the same time missing certain aspects of their old church while envisioning changes to this new one. I loved pastoring this flock, loved meeting people at their need places, loved ministering the truths of Scripture to them. Yet my heart focused constantly on giving my sweet unchurched friends a way into the church building, and the things I had tried simply didn't work.

Right after Christmas, Deb and I threw a Super Bowl party for my blues bar buddies. This time, 60 people showed up, a little more relaxed now, a little more trusting. Some brought their children. The blues bar waitress had become an avid gatherer of people. "Oh, you better be at Pastor Al's house or else, and yes, I'm talkin' to you!" It was again a sweet time — light on religion, but with a simple prayer for God's blessings and presence. Three people separately asked me for prayers.

But my actual church was still struggling, more and more. Finally a dear, longtime friend, one of the church elders, said the unthinkable: "We need to sell this building." It zapped me like the shock I got as a child, when I put my finger in a Christmas tree light socket on a dare. But this was even less fun. Seven acres, 13,000 square feet, stained glass windows and vaulted ceilings. We had worked so hard for it, sweat and worry and prayers, and then the victory celebrations. Was all this effort for naught? This was something bigger than I could process. I went to the blues bar and I started to rock, trying to find my center, as the singer launched into the great B.B. King song, "Nobody loves me but my mother".

Several weeks passed. The waitress asked me about Easter service. Oh right, the crowning day of the Christian faith! But I was too exhausted to find any passion. By now I had preached over 25 Easter sermons, all lost somewhere in my office files. I mumbled that all would be welcome at our church and please come, said in a pastor's recorded voice. Soon enough, word came back: pretty much nobody would come to the church. There were lots of jokes — that lightning would strike them, about needing larger glasses for communion, about fear of being converted. And there were other, whispered comments: they want your money; churches are like sales booths, once you go in you can't get out. "Why would I go there to learn to be a hypocrite when I'm already one?"

It all brought back my own wounded memories of being in church as a child and hearing a pastor who said, "I told you so" at a time of crisis. Getting funny looks because of my clothes or my haircut, or not knowing the protocol. The shame surrounding divorce, the fear of hellfire and brimstone, and feeling unable to measure up to the God-people's standards. What could I say to reassure my new friends, who all had their own wounded memories? One dear soul, the best smoker and drinker in the place, summed it all up. She put her arm around my neck and slurred, "Al, I already know I'm a loser, so I don't need to go to your church to hear that from you."

Their community was the people around them in the blues bar, people who were honest about their pain and troubles — not the church. Each week the blues faithful would come in, hug one another for real, and buy each other a few rounds. Then they would sit for a few hours, quietly murmuring "yep" to the lyrics of hardship a-coming again.

Then the waitress (darnit) spoke up again as she bounced by, "Hey, you could have your service here!"

"Right," I thought. Let's hold Easter service in a dirty, vomit-from-Saturday-night place where people would mock God and make their jokes about faith. What would I tell Deb? Even though I often find the jokes funny, sometimes my defenses kick in. Don't people understand there's a line that shouldn't be crossed? Don't they know that I need to defend God's name? The truth is, God can handle Himself just fine. God can handle the mysterious tension of fake mockery and real mocking, while hunting for a soul's salvation all the time. This God, I realized, could feel right at home in a blues bar.

I had a dear friend in the bar that I'll call Diane, a lawyer in her day job. Diane was the person who could talk to the owner about getting the place ready. So I asked her about this idea, and she immediately responded. "Are you freakin' crazy?"

The next morning, I was sitting in my other bar (Starbucks) when my phone rang. Diane asked me, "Al, did you do some freakin' voodoo thing to me?" "Sure," I said, "tell me which spell it was that worked on you?" Yes, Diane was up for organizing the Easter service. And she did it. She got the bar fixed up, hired a cleaner, gathered Easter crafts for the children, found a bunch of musicians, put banners up with crosses throughout the bar, and brought in 20 bundles of flowers to decorate the tables and the permanently sticky bar. She even organized a potluck lunch to follow the service, setting up plywood tops and tablecloths on the pool tables and sending out invitations. She worked like a dog.

On Easter Sunday, 75 people came in, with mixed fear and delight showing on their faces. Someone asked, "Are we really doing Easter here? Can this be a good thing, Pastor Al?" I had graduated from "Priest" to "Al" and now to "Pastor Al", which was okay, too.

10

People came all dressed up, some in collared shirts and simple dresses, some dressed fancier for church. I sensed a fear in the room about what I would say. Would it be about hell fire and brimstone, the old bait and switch trick? Would I make them feel guilty? Would I maybe call for a decision right in front of their friends? I noticed the lingering hugs and the whispers. I prayed I would stay on mission, a mission still in its discovery phase.

I preached my sermon on, "What resurrection are you counting on?" Is it about finding your soul mate? Getting your kids to turn out right? Finding the perfect job? Getting your health all fixed? I then made a case for Jesus, who died for sinners like Pastor Al and rose again, and is preparing a place for us to live with Him.

In the midst of speaking the message, I felt God's pleasure. It felt as if I loved these dear souls *with* God, in that moment with my new buddies. I had preached that morning in the church building, to the regular church folks, but the afternoon was for the blues group. Both were very real, both had precious people present, both had the resurrection story. But the blues music people made me feel God's pleasure in a more real way.

When I finished speaking, one of the musicians, a bass player, began to sing "Amazing Grace" in his gravelly, broken-by-life voice. He sang as if he desperately needed that song, that morning. The whole room shifted, from fearful to a softened soul. Something had shifted in me as well, and forever. This was a kind of evangelism that brought with it some new thoughts and habits and a transformation of my soul. Were these people my buddies first and foremost, and "targets" for evangelism sometime later?

The clear truth is that we have found a commitment to one another. On a recent Sunday, the bar owner had a question for me. She was excited about the plans for our Christmas service and party, and she asked if everyone could bring cookies. A new reality made itself clear. **We are not a church that meets in a blues bar. We are a blues bar that meets for church.**

All my life people have told me I was a good listener, but the truth is, I usually listened to reply. I was trained to reply. In fact, Western Christianity is built on "having an answer and giving a reply." Having a reply proved my spirituality, my pastoral credentials, and my intellect — right? But this dark and gritty little blues bar had taught me something else. It taught me *listening to hear*. I would sit there and listen for my own hurt to be spoken in the blues lyrics sung on stage. The people at the blues bar were all, like me, hearing their own thoughts, sorrows, and grievances in the blues lyrics. We were enough alike that we also heard each other in the sound of the blues.

This new adventure of mine was not in Africa or somewhere in the Pacific. I had found comfort — even found a home — as a missionary to an unreached group near my own church. I had to learn, and I continue to learn, their customs, taboos, and hang-ups, while I am still learning about my own.

I invite you to venture with me into the pages ahead. I suspect it will be a bit uncomfortable. You may find yourself asking, "Where is *my* blues bar? Do I ever interact in any meaningful way with any unchurched people? Does my church draw unbelievers into sustained, committed Christian fellowship? When I evangelize, do I talk or do I listen?"

What I can say with a fair amount of certainty from my experience and research is this: Something has changed for evangelism, something huge. The Judeo-Christian ethic is a foreign concept to most of your average folk outside the church. The unchurched world is filled with uncertainty and cynicism rules. People are not seeking Truth inside church buildings any more. In fact, most people don't believe there *is* such a thing as absolute truth.

I believe that the core truths of the Christian faith are as real and true today as they ever were. But we have lost our stride with evangelism, trying to share our faith. We think we know where the unchurched think, hunt, hide, and shop, and we design our seeker services to lure them in. But are we so busy designing our "lures" that we fail to get into the fishing boat, push away from shore, and brave the weather to be fishers of men *where the fish are*? Dance teachers talk about "dancing in the wild," which just means taking what you learned in the dance studio and trying it out on the dance floor of some restaurant or bar on a Friday night. The teachers know that many students will not venture beyond the safety of the ballroom studio where everyone does their practicing, and into a setting where the dance partner may make some unexpected moves. These chapters are based on my experiences fishing, and dancing, in the wild. They have deepened my love for the dance studio, the predictable, comfortable church world, and at the same time fueled my passion for adventures in the wild.

So, are you ready to take a risk with me? Are you wondering if your own inner wrestling with how to winsomely bring people to Jesus might find some answers in the pages ahead?

Take a quiet seat in the back of my blues bar, and listen in.

Chapter 2

It's All about Suffering (Not Just Apologetics)

"Born under a bad sign
I been down since I began to crawl...
Hard luck and trouble is my only friend...
My whole life has been one big fight."

-Albert King "Born Under a Bad Sign"

I was hiding in my blues bar, listening to Albert King's "Born Under a Bad Sign". I could hear in its mournful words the haunting moan of the original curse of humanity. Albert King got it. He felt it, he traveled with it in his nightmares, and maybe he lived it. The tortured, booming blues sound retold the story of Adam, of all of us, locked out of Paradise. I try to imagine that angel, who was created to protect and bless Adam, gripping the sword to be used on God's first-created human, if he didn't vacate the premises! The same story many of my blues people experience, through court judgments and restraining orders.

We don't know much about Albert King's early life. His father was a priest, who left the family of 13 children when Albert King was five years old. Pretty much all we know is what he captured in his perilous sounds. The lyrics were too-close-for-comfort and performed alongside the sweaty blues performances. He, too, was no doubt a traveler who could tell his own story of being locked out of paradise, of the times when the soul can't suppress its rage: "What's wrong with this world?"

I get that journey. I've been on it my whole life, and maybe you have too. My parents rose from their brokenness, but still, to some degree, they passed it on to me — the feeling of being a misfit in a world full of glossy advertisements, beckoning to a shiny new brand of life. Often as I preached from the pulpit about God's forgiveness and free grace, I was in a personal tailspin about my position in God's universe.

How I got here

My pain has a history; it starts with a pivotal moment. While God knows the entirety of my story, with the generations stretching all the way back to Adam, I find one particular moment that haunts me, and that I believe has shaped my life and my ministry. It begins with a man named Murray Gillespie, my grandfather.

Murray was born in 1920 in Quebec, Canada — one of seven children born to Annie Gillespie. Annie was married to a sea captain, who often came home drunk and in a rage. The family could only find so many places to hide from his anger. Annie was known for her cooking, and the one safe place for the seven children was her love-made food. One night the captain came home in a drunken rage, threw a lighted lantern and burned down the family home. This was the world - and the family - in which Murray grew up.

As an adult, Murray lived in Baltimore, Maryland, part of a working class defined by the clanging, loud sounds of people hammering, hauling, and welding things. Murray and his neighbors worked hard, punched their time cards in and out, and drank beer to soothe their aching muscles and forget about the long, monotonous workday.

This was maybe 1955. Dwight D. Eisenhower was still president. The first official advisors were sent to Vietnam, and Ray Kroc opened his first McDonald's in Des Plaines, Illinois. Hurricane Diane hit the northeast United States, killing 200 people and causing over $1 billion in damage. Rosa Parks was arrested for refusing to give up her seat on a bus to a white person, and the national civil rights movement began.

That same year, Murray Gillespie jumped from a smoke-blackened bridge into the path of an oncoming train. Alcoholism, adultery, unemployment, separation from his children, and the wounds of his own childhood had pressed down on his soul. No pastor, no apologetic was there to reason with him and shift his decision. I suppose his last thought might have been, "Just get this endless suffering cycle over with." He died with no one present. I heard this story as a child, and over the years I have imagined, hundreds of times, his body hitting the front of a speeding train.

16

Murray Gillespie left two children: Hope, and Murray Jr. He named his daughter after a grandmother he loved, and by the time she was 12 (the year he died) he had written her three letters. The letters were the only real connection that Hope ever had with her father. That sweet, young, fatherless Hope is my mother.

The spiral of anger, alcohol, drugs, pornography, and an endless list of addictions formed a kind of loop in the movie of our family, always playing in a new theatre. As a child, Hope was shuffled around Baltimore between wherever her grandmother was living and her mother's raging, "yell-all-night" home that offered few safe places to hide. She was often in charge of her four half brothers and sisters. It wasn't pretty. When Hope was 13, one of the "rich" boys invited Hope to a party at his house. I should mention that Hope had one bold, shocking gift: she was gorgeous, though she didn't know it. Men would gawk, employers would open a path, and a jealous mother would try to sabotage her.

Well, Hope got pregnant by the rich boy, and his father offered her $500 to make the abortion happen. Hope didn't know what "abortion" meant, and when the doctor told her, she refused. The doctor promised Hope that she would be given the address of the foster parents' home after the birth. But after the baby — my older brother — was born, Hope went into a coma for nine days. She was too weak to see the baby for three months, but she finally found the baby and took him home.

Things went from bad to hell bad. At the age of 15, Hope left her mother's home, invested a quarter in a newspaper, found an apartment, lied about her age, and showed up for a job interview at the Stiff Silver Company. Her photos as a young woman resemble the pictures of Lucille Ball from the 1920s; the gift of beauty helped to open doors, which always mystified her. She was soon put in charge of leading busloads of tourists around the factory and explaining how each department worked. Her job responsibilities grew, and before long she was making $42 a week — an amount that, for a 15-year-old who had lied about her age, represented unknown security, a dreamscape experience. She had a single driving motive: to have a home of her own for herself and her baby.

Then a man moved into the room across the hall from her tiny apartment. He was a foreigner, clearly older than she was, and clearly interested. Hope avoided him, always hurrying in and out of her door.

Her experience was that men die or they abuse you, or both. The man persisted, knocking on her door to ask her out. Unable to fend him off, she simply moved out the first time he went on a trip. She wrote him a note: "Please don't look for me," explaining that he was too old for her. It took him three months to find her, and he pursued her until she finally relented and agreed to marry him.

What was he like? Did he treat her well? Did she secretly like him? Or was she just too worn down to refuse him? The pastor and his wife were the only ones in attendance. The groom brought the marriage certificate; it showed his age as 36 years old, divorced, and Hope's age as 16. Hope protested that she was only 15, but she signed the paper. She was by now in a full anxiety attack, and the groom actually said her vows for her.

That man was my father, also named Al; I was born shortly thereafter.

Hope still wrestled with a life that gave her so few options and little space for self-expression, while her marriage got tougher. That film loop of her grandfather's and her parents' stories seemed destined to make its ugly return. Hope's marriage started out as the same story: constant fighting, late nights and lost time, adultery and addictions — until something unexpected arrived in the mail. It was a tract from the Oliver B. Greene ministry that explained how to become a Christian. Hope prayed the prayer, and a new journey began, one with its own bumps and landmines.

By the time she was 22, Hope had five children with Al. But now, with her new faith, she had started a new family story. The five little lives had moved her, urged her, to find meaning for those children, something that she had never known. And she managed to bring my father along on her journey.

Pain lifts the veil

I often hear people complain, talking about church people, about the "happy, happy, happy" image we project. C.S. Lewis put his finger on the answer: "Pain removes the veil; it plants the flag of truth." (*The Problem of Pain*) I have told you my history so that you can fully understand my pain, which I no longer try to hide. We honestly do not need to channel those singing *Double-mint* twins, from the 1970s commercials, who banished their troubles with chewing gum as they frolicked, never blinking, in the sunshine. How often have I tried to "sell" Jesus with a happy jingle, suppressing my own blues tune — fearful that my own sorrows and demons might expose my weaknesses and undermine the sales pitch?

But the unchurched are not buying the happy pitch; it doesn't square with the bad-luck life they are living. My blues buddies were seasoned life travelers and they didn't mind telling me off: "F*** the church" and "f*** your GOD- D***** Christianity!" Or they ask, in many ways and states of mind, "Where was your God when my child was taken from me?"

One day, Lester stopped into the blues bar for the first time. When he heard the waitress call me Pastor Al — I had given up trying to stop her — he turned and challenged me: why the f*** was I in a blues bar anyway? He quickly apologized for his "French" — but he was seriously upset. "My God-d***** wife left me tonight, threw all my clothes in the dumpster and took our car. And to top off my evening I have to sit next to you! F*** this, I'm gone! Oh, and God bless you, Pastor Al." Lester had no emotional space for unwanted encounters because his pain had used up all his reserves. The kind of pain that makes an animal caught in a trap chew its own leg off to find freedom — freedom without a leg.

I did not grow up in a *Double-mint* commercial, and neither did many or most of the Christians I know. The suicide of my grandfather was only two thoughts away, and there was discord in all the relationships around me. I remember the year when I was preaching a series of sermons on making a "Biblical Marriage" — in a season when Deb and I were not in a good place in our own relationship. Deb served in the Sunday school that year, just so I wouldn't have to meet her eyes in the sanctuary as I offered my message of hope. Evangelism offers a little more cover: it's most often one or two conversations with a stranger, never threatening the crooked places in my soul. But speaking in church on Sunday to the parishioners who come every week presents a challenge if you have a few truths you'd prefer to hide. So, we perfect a kind of dualism, a contrast between the life we really live and the life we present in our "witnessing monologues." We aren't telling the whole truth, and perhaps our motives are even hidden from ourselves. Perhaps we feel the need to hide from our own stories. The real, unstoppable human storyline is loss.

Loss is in fact our oldest storyline, with its roots back in Genesis 3:

> Cursed is the ground because of you; through painful
> toil you will eat food from it all the days of your life.
> It will produce thorns and thistles for you, and you
> will eat the plants of the field.
> By the sweat of your brow you will eat your food
> until you return to the ground, since from it you were
> taken; for dust you are and to dust you will return.

It's not simply the perplexity that drives us to God — it's the hurts. It's our aching questions that show us His eyes and His arms open to us, and His Son suffering on the cross. The soul feels all the hurt of our great fall and is driven to seek God. And this is pain's purpose. C.S. Lewis puts it this way: "Pain insists on being attended to. God whispers to us in our pleasures, speaks in our consciences, but shouts in our pains. It is his megaphone to rouse a deaf world." (*The Problem of Pain*)

Seminary students, for over a century, have been trained in the power of apologetics, studying the many reasons for turning to God. Apologetics surely have value, and for those willing to engage their work, they present a compelling case for belief in the God of the Bible. But might this be a smaller part of the evangelism landscape than we think? In my 25 years as a pastor, I have learned that the ways of the soul are cryptic and deep. A theological, well-reasoned answer rarely ministers to the unbeliever as deeply as being present with them in their questions and pain.

That is why I propose that the turnstile of evangelism today must pivot not on apologetics but on human suffering. Of course, scholars have not disregarded suffering in studying the soul's track to God. But now, the soul's crisis needs to take center stage. The world today seems to be crying out, "If your God is so great, why is my life so d*** bad?" But the secret hope is buried somewhere, the hope that it's all true — that we can meet our Creator somehow. The big questions cycle in our souls every day: "Where did I come from?" "What am I doing here?" "What happens after death?" And our suffering seems to point us away from faith in God: "This God does not like me much because my life is so tough. Why does He assign this homework of suffering?"

One evening in the blues bar, after I had been *outed* as a pastor, one man challenged me — not to give him answers, but to listen. "If you all would just shut the hell up," he said, "maybe you could hear what we have to say about our lives." I answered, "Tell me more." He then shared with me his own long cycle of suffering, admitting that he had never told anyone this before. I was glad to see him, later, at the Easter service we held in the blues bar.

There he would hear another great, true story about suffering. In Luke 23, Jesus suffers more than any human being ever will. But in the midst of his own unspeakable suffering, He speaks to the crucified thief who is without hope, lost in his pain. The thief begs him, "Jesus, remember me when you come into your kingdom." Jesus answers, "Truly, I tell you, today you will be with me in paradise." A ray of hope pierces the darkness when we realize that Jesus has not forgotten who we are.

We are heard, remembered, and redeemed at the point where the promise of eternity, bought by Christ on the cross, breaks the temporal time loop. There is hope for us, that we can have eternity itself set alongside our real temporal suffering. The blues lyrics of Joe Cocker echo within our own souls, and the souls of those around us: "Don't forget me, please don't forget me." I suspect that the first step as we connect with the unchurched is to simply hear and acknowledge their questions, pain, and suffering, and to listen even more carefully to the questions our own soul is asking. Perhaps it is time for us to recognize that our pain is what makes us human, and to become more transparent in our suffering. We are all broken, and we are all seeking our Creator.

Maybe it's time for us to reconsider the thinking of the unchurched. They, like we, are created in the image of God. Each person's inner soul wrestles with the image of his Creator, pondering the universal human questions: "Where did I come from?" "Why am I here?" "Where do I go after death?" Evangelists must listen well, listen with the heart as well as the head, in order to hear these deeper questions.

I'd like to challenge you to do a little exercise. The next time you engage in a conversation with someone that has a point of view different than your own, see if you can observe your own "front narrative" and "back narrative". The "front narrative" is the audible conversation and exchange of spoken ideas. The "back narrative" is what is going on in our heads. It is the internal process of introspecting, evaluating, and shaping our responses. This is where we strategize, judge the other person's thoughts and feelings, and ready our reply. When we interact with the unchurched, how many of us are on the defensive, a bit nervous and off-balance as we seek to craft just the right response to this "lost soul"? In our eagerness to present our airtight case, how many of us miss hearing the subtext of what the other person is saying? Are we able to be quiet long enough to find a connection to the real person, rather than to counter his thoughts and experiences?

In the blues bar one Sunday night, a man in his sixties came and sat near me. He looked a little stiff and out of place; maybe he wanted to be in hiding for a few hours. In church, of course, I would walk around and greet people, and I was expected to do so, but here in the bar, leaving people alone was expected. So I let him be. A bit later, when someone I knew came in, he introduced us, and then he whispered to me: "Steve lost both his wife and daughter to cancer two months ago." Thunderstruck, I began to cry quietly. Feeling his pain - sharing his pain - was my first step toward him.

Ann Voskamp, grappling with her own journey through pain and towards God, says in her book *The Broken Way*, "Somehow I wonder if it's in shattered places, with broken people, we are most near the broken heart of Christ." (32). Perhaps - just perhaps - we need to spend more time with brokenness. Maybe one of the first steps in evangelism is to be willing to feel our own pain, so that we can also be present as we share the pain of others.

Chapter 3

We Are Not Present

"This is a mean old world, baby, to live in by yourself....
I drink to keep from worrying, baby, I smile to keep
from crying..."

T. Bone Walker "Mean Old World"

Thank God for the moms who organize those father- daughter dances, the ones who make centerpieces all glitter and sparkles, who dim the room just right for self-conscious "couples," who set out the little paper plates and matching cups. They know how to create a space for that awkward but enchanting daddy-daughter dance — encouraging men who, in their day job, might be writing top-secret code for a military satellite, to actually dance and mingle.

Each year from the time our daughters entered first grade up until their eighth grade year, my friend Jeff and I would huddle in a corner, make fun of each other, and then go out on the floor and dance with our daughters. They, of course, were beaming with little girl beauty: a beauty we wished, in our old dad hearts, would never, never change. Coming into this setting was like waking up in a bowl of *Jello* — everything looked strange. But if I could, I would like to thank those ladies who gave me a whole file of treasured memories with my daughter.

Erin and I went to our dad and daughter dances for seven years. Each year she would start talking about outfits three months ahead. It took me a lot longer to realize that I needed to contemplate clothing. I was familiar with a variety of clothes: I had a bright orange outfit for when I went deer hunting; I would outfit my duffle bag with a floppy hat (along with a venom extraction kit) before going on a mission trip to Africa. Unfortunately, these outfits would not work for this occasion. I finally asked Erin for help. Who could have known that my "outfit" should in some way match her outfit? Fathers are like Captain America: we will rise to defeat any evil that could cause our little girl even a moment of fear — even fear of a fashion disaster. But Erin rescued us both. She picked out my black suit and black shoes, plus a tie that matched the color of her dress.

Erin and I rode together in my old truck to the dance. In the passenger's seat next to me was one of the two precious children I was given in this life. Now eight years old, wearing a flower brooch on her dress, she was battling with the seat belt and trying to get settled. In little girls, God brought beauty into the world, and sitting here next to me was God doing His best art. So, why was my mind so far away, embroiled in its own conflict? This was one of those times I was trying not to pray for someone I truly hated. I was thinking about all his faults and offenses, picturing myself winning our epic debate, seeing this difficult person punished for the wrongs he did. Even as a pastor, is any of us immune to anger, jealousy, and even deep hatred? I have to admit that a black, dungeon-like moment was brewing inside of me.

Then, breaking in as if from far away, I heard Erin's voice challenging me. "Dad. Dad, are you there? DAD? DAD?!! Where are you?" I had completely lost awareness of where I was, and whom I was with. I had lost sight of this rare moment. Captain America was driving the truck but totally oblivious, despite his fancy shield and matching socks. At one of the most precious moments my short life on earth could offer, I had gone missing. I had fallen into a dungeon and couldn't get myself out.

For me, this was a bellwether moment, when I realized I had traded something so big for something so trivial. Even ten years later, my mind often drifts to this teaching moment. How many of us, in our lonely old age, might pine silently over the lost opportunity to take our little girl to a dance?

At other moments, too, we are not always present with the people God has brought into our lives. Some of these are people that He wants us to share our faith with, and we miss the opportunity to truly connect with them. For me, the question arises: If we are not present in those moments of evangelism, where are we?

Driving to the dance, I was present in my anger instead of with my daughter. As busy 21st-century people, there are many places our minds can travel to. But I suspect we may be in our pain, in our own fear, or even in our theology and our scripts, instead of in the gospel.

We are in our pain

I was a brand-new driver, 17 years old. I saw the car in front of me swerve to the left, lurch as if it had hit a speed bump, swerve back to the right, and speed off. Few cars were around on this country road. It was dark and hard to see, so I stopped in the middle of the road. Something was lying in the road, something scary and out of a horror movie. I wanted to just drive off and not look at what was there in the road; I still wish I had. Someone's dog was lying in the road, half-crushed from the speeding car, on its way to a terrible, slow death.

Ours was an animal-loving family; we had goldfish and 1500-pound steers and everything in between. I would say that I lived in a zoo. And really mean I lived in a zoo! My mother was a living, breathing Dr. Doolittle! The sight of this suffering dog tore my heart out.

The large dog had a collar, which meant an owner — someone who cared for him. When I tried to comfort the dog, he snapped like a harpooned alligator, barely missing me. But the pain had used up all the cells in his half-alive body. Now I heard someone. A middle-aged couple was walking out from the lawn nearby. It was their dog, and I was the person with the car at the scene of this horrific moment. I'm beginning to cry as I write this, remembering the woman's cry, the saddest noise I had ever heard. It looked as if I was the driver who had hit their dog, who continued to writhe in sickening pain. After a minute the man dragged his sobbing wife away; she was hitting him. Another neighbor showed up with a gun and quickly shot the dog in the head. Silence. He looked at me and said, "You can go son; things happen."

I never actually told them it wasn't me. I didn't want to bring everyone more pain, and I was just hoping to forget. But that's not how our mind behaves, of course. I went to my math class the next morning, and I couldn't focus. The numbers were blurred on the page. In woodshop (my favorite class) I couldn't focus either. I skipped lunch. Later that day I threw up, overwhelmed by the horror of what I had seen.

Just as the dog's whole being was consumed with physical pain, our minds can also be consumed with pain, sometimes physical, and sometimes other kinds. Our minds are consumed with conflicts we haven't laid to rest: conflicts between family members, job difficulties, our children's struggles with learning disabilities or other problems, a crazy health scare or a bad medical report, and all our other grim realities. The decibel level of the noise within our souls drowns out our ability to hear, perceive, and truly *live* within the present moment.

What uses up all the space where "being present" needs to be nurtured? Our pain does. Pain can use up all our extra space and push out the opportunity to grow a new relationship. Our minds continue to grind over our past marriages, the mental illness of a parent, loss of money (whether due to gambling or bad decisions or dumb luck), the disrespect that comes with being not smart enough or big enough or thin enough or pretty enough—on and on.

You know, the touch of the Savior's hands and words came to so many people who were in pain: the woman at the well; the blind man; the thief hanging on the cross. Their pain wasn't always resolved, but His presence made the pain bearable, even meaningful. He can turn down the volume of the noisy, hurting soul. As a child I can remember screaming like I was dying when I scraped my knee, but once Mom was there, the pain mattered less. Her knowing and caring got me back in motion, ready for my next skinned knee.

Once, when I was traveling in Florida, I was privileged to provide this caring presence. I was sitting in a chair near the beach, and a very attractive couple came and sat nearby. She was a beautiful Indian woman, wearing a— well—a bathing suit that only an Indian Beauty Princess was authorized to wear. The man was someone I could only describe as the Hulk, like the comic book character but without the green hue. His muscles had muscles, and then some. So here I am, sitting in a force field of beauty and strength that could not be charted. I've learned to appreciate God's humor, and I wondered if some divine appointment was possibly unfolding. I truly hoped not.

Looking at her would do something to me, and looking at him could end my life fast.

Anxiously aware of this powerful man beside me, unexpected words came out of my mouth: "Dude, I'm not even looking at her."

He laughed and said, "No problem, man."

This was good, now I was free to sit quietly and keep to myself. Then he asked, "Where are you from?"

"Virginia," I answered. He was quiet for some time, and then said, "My dad was from Virginia."

"Does he still live there?"

"No; he died last year."

"I'm sorry, my friend."

The hulk started to cry, and I said, "Tell me more." He recounted how his father had been such a jackass his whole life, and he had just died, at 57 years old.

"I never told him goodbye, I'm sorry for being such an idiot [he used more colorful words], and I never told him I loved him."

The Indian princess stopped putting on lotion and took off her sunglasses.

I'm not sure why, but the words that came out of my mouth were: "I sense God feels your pain and cries too."

The hulk gave me this look, like a child who needs to cry, but can't. And then he just put his hand on my shoulder and sobbed. The Indian princess became a statue. He said, "Are you a religious guy or something?" I said I was a Christian working my way through life as God showed me the way. Then came the words. "You know, I hate it when people give me advice I don't ask for; you're the first religious guy to not tell me what to do and then just repeat it every time I see them." His wife then invited me to an Indian dinner at their home, next time I was in town.

God had given me a gift, in allowing an authentic, free-flowing work of the Holy Spirit to take place with that Indian princess and the broken Hulk.

We are in our fears

At five, I remember fearing the impending arrival of my younger brother or sister. Where would it sleep? Whose food would it eat?

How long would it stay in our house? At age seven, I was worried sick that I couldn't be Spiderman at Halloween. The Spiderman outfit laid waiting in a box under the steps, but in our house, it was first-come first-served to the costume box. At 12 years old I feared I would stay short forever: wrestling in the 98-pound weight class in 8th grade, I was a real chick magnet (not!). At 16 my fears were a bit more serious. I feared having no escape from my parents' home. The thought that I would live there till I was 17 was unthinkable!

As an adult, fear unfortunately did not go away. My Hebrew teacher in seminary struck fear into me like no one ever had. I often thought, "I could take this guy with one hand tied around my ankle" — but that never helped my grade. More than anything else, I feared he would say, "Mr. Dayhoff will be reading for us today." It was like living in the movie *Dumb and Dumber*.

That was before fear really arrived in my life. I became a father. Wesley bounced into our lives when Deb and I were in our late 20s. I worried constantly; every night I would go into his room to see if he was breathing. I had read all the advice about putting kids on their backs or their stomachs (or maybe letting them free range in the backyard?). I couldn't sleep till I saw his little chest moving. Knowing Wesley, I imagine he would have held his breath on purpose if he thought I was watching. The fear plagued my thoughts and kept me from sleep.

Fears follow every age in life. They grow with us, like moles on our skin. Similar fears stalk all of us, ruling over us in our weak moments. Fear has had sway in my own life-space, far too much. And it keeps us from being *present*, because fear, like a self-absorbed child, demands to be the center of attention. But the Lord never intended us to live in fear, and the Scriptures teach us that fear cripples the soul. 1 John 4:8 reads, "There is no fear in love. But perfect love drives out fear, because fear has to do with punishment. The one who fears is not made perfect in love."

I remember the time I saw a bird fly through an open door and into our home, when I was about 10 years old. A ten-year-old boy watches with mischievous delight as a free-for-all unfolds at such rare, wonderful moments. My mom was deathly afraid of birds flying in the house. Add two little sisters, and you've got a scene like the running of the bulls in Spain. I sat in sheer happiness appreciating how a little bird could herd and terrify everyone, creating chaos, a spastic flying around of legs and arms. You couldn't pay for this kind of entertainment! But to those terrified, fear controls us and steals our ability to function. We become panicked and paralyzed as our fears overwhelm us.

To hear our Savior's voice and feel His touch begins with understanding our weaknesses, naming our fears, and acknowledging our inability to move forward on our own. It is not in our own strength that we swat the fears away — His love does the work for us. Love does for us what we cannot do for ourselves.

At one of my evangelism seminars, I asked the people around the table, "What do you fear about evangelism?" The answers they gave were stunningly honest. They feared conflict and rejection. They were afraid they were lying, that they were creating confusion, that they would fail. And they were afraid that someone would discover the mess in their own lives and families. How do we find a way to accept our own fears and failings, so we can be more present with the people with whom we are talking?

We are in our theology

I recently went to a blues festival in Wheeling, WV. It was a delightful setting, the performers' stage set off by the backdrop of the Ohio River. I listened to blues while watching people fish. Such simple joy, baby! But in front of the stage stood the inevitable security guys, big mean men in skin-tight t-shirts with bulging biceps. They were there to intimidate, to create a barrier between eager fans and the sought-after musicians. As I watched them, I was reminded of the Pharisees of Jesus' day, the self-appointed gate-keepers to the kingdom of God.

I wonder if sometimes, unknowingly, we become "little Pharisees" in our evangelism. Are there ways that we intimidate unbelievers in our smug assurance of our theological correctness? Do we create barriers when we silently dismiss those whose lifestyles we find unacceptable? Do my well-articulated theological beliefs serve as a buffer between me and everyone else? Do I enjoy and feel safe in the self-assured position of being "more right" than others in my life?

Many of my friends from the blues bar carry baggage from their experiences with "Christians" at some point in their journey. It may be a parent, a sibling, an aunt or uncle, a pastor. But the wounds all bear a resemblance; a disconnect exists between *faith talk they heard and the hypocrisy they saw.* We all struggle with this to one extent or another. Whether in our own lives, or in the relationships around us, we know that the brokenness that we see doesn't square with the God-talk and religious posturing. Maybe we simply need to be more honest, both with ourselves and with our unbelieving friends.

Perhaps we are prone to position ourselves in our theology, rather than simply experience and be attentive to the unique human beings God has placed in our lives.

In my journey of seeking the unchurched person's perspective, I often hear people cite the "religion routine" they inherited from their parents as a significant stumbling block in their journey to faith.

I think of my friend, "Ben." His parents got divorced early in life, and the inevitable question came: "What should we do with this child our failed marriage made?" The divorce was so painful, and the child such a reminder of the disastrous union, that they decided to send him away to boarding school. It was a prestigious "solution" to a "mistake" that arose from intimacy. Ben spent his life reciting the theological underpinnings given to him by his parents. Yet, it was very clear to me that he simply wanted his parents' presence in his ordinary life journey. He always made them proud with grades and athletic accomplishments, and then his deep, introspective gaze would sometimes tear away the curtain to reveal the real narrative. He wanted them to be present.

Ben's family was a family of faith. Their story, I think, speaks to a disturbing trend among Christians. Many have been marginalized and depersonalized by a mentor who was strong in their theology (maybe a father, mother, sibling, or teacher) but weak in relational grace — and they pass on that same marginalizing attitude in their network of God-given relationships. How many of us have drifted into observing the mechanics of our faith without experiencing its energy, its presence in God's shockingly beautiful creation? Do we miss the wonders of a loving God who is busy preparing a place for us for when our labors here on earth are over? As God delighted in walking in the Garden of Eden with Adam & Eve, he was feeding the relationship with His very presence. Theology is meant to create a presence, not shield us from the intimate contact of being with other people.

We are in our scripts

I am convinced that God can use anything, anyone, anytime, anywhere to initiate faith and salvation in any soul. Can God use a child's spontaneous observations to call a mom to faith? Sure. Can God use the sunset, in all its beauty from the window of a New York skyscraper, to redeem a blind man? Yep. Can God use the hallucinogenic high of a cocaine user to see, feel, and argue himself to faith? Uh huh. God can use the most pathetic and poorly- formed gospel proposals, and He can choose not to anoint the clearest gospel speech ever heard. It's God that provides the power to save and awaken a soul.

Having said all that, I come from the era of Christian scripts. Thank God for them! They are well intentioned and, at times, very effective. The Roman Road, The Four Spiritual Laws, the Bridge Illustration, the Evangelism Explosion question ("If God were to say, 'Why should I let you into my heaven?' what would you say?"). Please hear that I fully believe all of these can be helpful tools to introduce the gospel to peoples' hearts and minds. However, I think something has changed. In a culture where people no longer accept "truth" as a relevant concept - and in fact where they are offended by the idea of anything approaching "absolute truth" - our scripted questions sound more like contrived talking points.

It's when we get a question that we haven't been trained to answer that the cracks begin to show. People are onto the "sales pitch," the recording, a trained approach, a script. One person in my blues bar network turned to me and said, "Oh, I've heard that a million times. That's all you got?"

But we have to say *something*, right? We have to use words in a certain order or logic to communicate the gospel, don't we?

Matthew 16:13–20 gives us an exchange of Jesus with the disciples:

> When Jesus came to the region of Caesarea Philippi, he asked his disciples, "Who do people say the Son of Man is?" They replied, "Some say John the Baptist; others say Elijah and still others, Jeremiah or one of the prophets." "But what about you?" he asked. "Who do you say I am?" Simon Peter answered, "You are the Messiah, the Son of the living God."

What is interesting is that, up to this point, Jesus allowed long spaces of time to flow by without ever instructing the disciples on who He was. The key moment came when Jesus turned to the disciples and asked, "Who do you say that I am?" It took a long time of being present with the disciples to lead up to the acid question.

Scripts can be useful, and we know that generations benefited from them. But they will be most useful when they are used in a moment of being truly present with a person. And they will only be useful when prompted by the nudging of the Holy Spirit saying, "It's time".

Being present

Marina Abramovic is a Serbian-born, New York-based performance artist who describes herself as "the grandmother of performance art." Her art explores the relationship between performer and audience, the limits of the body, and how communication can happen or be prevented. From March 14 to May 31, 2010, the Museum of Modern Art in NYC held a major presentation of Abramovic's work—the biggest exhibition of performance art in MoMA's history. During the run of the exhibition, Abramovic performed "The Artist is Present" — a 736- hour static, silent piece, in which she sat immobile in the museum's atrium, while spectators were invited to take turns sitting opposite her. The program broke attendance records, attracting more than 850,000 visitors.

During the exhibit, some people came and stood in line 10 times to sit with her; one man sat with her looking into her eyes for seven hours. Person after person after person stood in line for hours to experience a still, silent connection with Marina, in the sterile setting of a museum with hundreds looking on. People described a spiritual experience, something they have never had before, but longed for. Maybe it was the need to be seen, or the need for a space where the unspoken communication could be heard, as if loud and articulate. Maybe many craved the attention of someone who would simply be quiet and be with them, even as hundreds looked on. How did so many people manage to be "alone with Marina" in that setting? Being present with someone, having a core that is quiet and at rest, has its own inaudible connection. This begins to define the spiritual encounter with God.

There are videos of Marina Abramovic on YouTube that show clearly the simple but profound skill of being present with someone. Many begin to cry after just a few minutes — maybe because, for the first time, they feel valuable enough to have another person look at them, directly and deeply, examining the story in their eyes and exhibiting no fear, in this human encounter that is slow, unfolding, and full of unscripted surprises.

The exhibition had such a deep impact on the participants that a support group for the "sitters," Sitting With Marina, was established on Facebook, complete with its own blog. Questions swirled around this art presentation: What was it? Why did so many people come again and again? How could one person sitting in silence with another have such dramatic impact on so many people? Sitting silent, how hard could that be? As hard as raising the Titanic out of frigid water, apparently. The people who sat opposite Marina described the experience as life changing, the unzipping of the soul, being seen by someone, finally connecting with another human being.

Marina's knowledge of how to be present had been forged by a life of struggle, pain, and denial, of being invisible to key people in her life. What she had been denied, she learned to give to others, and she made it an art form. Marina demonstrated a simple, rare and life-changing moment: being truly present with someone.

Perhaps there is a side of us that communicates without words or scripts or proposals, feeding the starving souls of others in our lives. Perhaps it's about perceiving that the other person wants to be with you and isn't in a rush to get away from you. I believe much of Western evangelism is rooted in the notion of a stranger walking up to a stranger and initiating a conversation that challenges their worldview. This model provides *contact*, but no *connection.* Marina demonstrated a simple, rare and life-changing moment: being present with someone and thereby *establishing connection.*

We are not present. We are not present in the lives and minds of the people God has brought into our lives. The hidden truth is that this is a silent, devious cancer within the faith relationships that God has enabled us to pursue.

We desperately need to reclaim the holy ability of being present, fully and without fear, to those with whom we long to communicate the gospel.

Perhaps it is time for us - as individuals, as pastors, as a Christian community - to pause and ask ourselves: What is it that keeps us from being *truly present* with the unbelievers around us? Is it our own pain? Is it the tremendous fear of our own inadequacy, or rejection, or being discovered? Does our arrogant assurance of our theological superiority keep us from just *being* with people who are different from us? Are we so glued to the necessity of a script to follow that we dare not untether ourselves and breathe easily with people?

Amazing things await you, my friend. Be willing to risk. Listen carefully. Be *present* with the unbelievers around you. You will be astonished at the things you begin to hear when you truly listen.

Chapter 4

Our "Joseph" Story

"I went down to the crossroads, fell down on my knees,
I went down to the crossroads, fell down on my knees,
Asked the Lord above for mercy, 'Save me if you please'.
I went down to the crossroads, tried to flag a ride,
I went down to the crossroads, tried to flag a ride,
Nobody seemed to know me, everybody passed me by."

"Crossroads", Eric Clapton & BB King
(Lyrics: Robert Johnson)

Suppose that Gladys Love Smith had not met Vernon Presley in 1933, at the Evangelical First Assembly of God Church in East Tupelo. Why would that matter? Well, there would have been no Elvis Presley. When their eyes met at church, and a little ordinary, awkward conversation started between two young people, who could have imagined that a multi-billion-dollar industry would be the result? Elvis Presley has sold (it is estimated) more than one billion record units worldwide, more than any one other singer in record industry history. Elvis had 149 songs appear on Billboard's "Hot 100 Pop Chart" in America.

But there is another side to the story. Few know or remember about Jesse Garon Presley, Elvis's stillborn twin brother. How did the baby's death affect Gladys, Vernon, and Elvis? When he was growing up, Elvis heard a mysterious voice that he believed was his brother Jesse. Not much is known about how Elvis revisited the memory of his lost twin, nor how his parents grieved or contemplated Jesse's growing up years that never happened. But families everywhere can't stop asking "what if" about those taken too young. The story behind the story of Elvis Presley's life is fascinating, heart-breaking, and full of hidden secrets — perhaps hidden from Elvis himself.

Like it or not, your family is a central piece of the person you are now. I had a vivid reminder of this day walking toward a public bathroom. Just in front of me was an elderly World War II vet, beginning to struggle with the door handle. As I leaned forward to open the door for him I seemed to enter into his space — a comfortable space, furnished with the familiar buttoned plaid shirts and Old Spice aftershave that always reminded me of my own father. So, once we were inside and I saw him lose his balance while standing at the urinal, it was just second nature to reach out to steady him, and I held onto him until he had finished his errand. Then he turned to me and said simply, "Thank you soldier." No matter how long I live, I know that the WWII generation will stay in my memory: after all, God sent me to a soldier.

All families are great messy stories, waiting for some narrative to organize all the people, events, and experiences unique to our personal history. Family storytelling is so important to the next generation and the next. Genesis 45 contains one of the greatest, messy family stories contained in the Bible, the story of Joseph in embarrassing detail. It's the story of someone realizing where he had been sent in the past so that lives would be saved in the future. Family chaos, stolen dignity, mysterious meetings, and a rags-to-riches story worthy of a PBS special. Let's take a look.

Did God send Joseph into Egypt?

Joseph was the son of Jacob and his beloved wife, Rachel. Because he loved Rachel so much, Jacob showed partiality towards Joseph, fashioning for him a "coat of many colors" — an act that elevated his position and infuriated Jacob's other sons. Family jealousy ran rampant. Matters worsened when Joseph started having dreams. He dreamed that his brothers' sheaves of wheat bowed to his own sheaves, and he had the poor judgment to share this dream with his siblings. His second dream compounded their resentment, with the sun and moon and eleven stars also bowing before him. The account in Genesis 37 states that his brothers "hated him all the more" and that "his father rebuked him."

One day, amid this tension, Jacob sent Joseph out to check on his brothers working in the fields. The brothers, consumed with anger, looked for a way to get rid of him. Reuben, as the eldest, was responsible for the safety of his younger brothers, and he balked at the idea of killing Joseph outright. As a compromise he suggested that they throw him into a deep well. Some Midianite merchantmen happened by, and the decision to sell Joseph rather than let him die in the cistern spared his life but sealed his fate. The brothers then bloodied Joseph's pretty coat and agreed to tell Jacob that a wild animal had eaten him.

Having been sold into slavery, Joseph was eventually bought by Potiphar, the captain of Pharaoh's guard. "And the Lord was with Joseph" (Gen. 39:2). Stop . . . and let that phrase sink in. Joseph's life has devolved from favored and blessed son to hated, deserted, and now enslaved *nobody*. Yet Genesis 39 has the gall to state plainly, *"And the Lord was with Joseph."* Hmm . . . the Lord hasn't stepped in to halt any of the tragedy, has He?

In no time at all, Joseph proved his mettle, and Potiphar made him an overseer in his house. Potiphar delegated everything to Joseph except for the preparation of the food for Potiphar himself. However, Joseph's position was complicated by the actions of Potiphar's wife, trying day after day to persuade Joseph to "lie with her." Joseph repeatedly refused, out of respect for both Potiphar and God. Finally, Potiphar's wife lost patience and grabbed him. He fled, losing his garment, which she kept as evidence, and accused Joseph of trying to rape her, reminding Potiphar that he was the one who had "brought this slave" into their house.

The caliber of Joseph's integrity here is incredible. If anyone ever had legitimate reason to be a "victim," and therefore entitled to a little indulgence at the expense of his employer, it was Joseph. Yet Joseph takes the high road, and he pays a heavy price.

Potiphar could have had Joseph killed on the spot. Instead, he had Joseph thrown into prison. "And the Lord was with Joseph" (Gen. 39:21). There it is again! Joseph's stretch of apparent "bad luck" is stretching into *years* now. But the Scriptures insist *the Lord was with Joseph.*

Soon enough, Joseph was an overseer of the other prisoners: when Pharaoh's cupbearer and his baker were thrown into prison, Joseph was assigned to be responsible for them. When they both had disturbing dreams, Joseph was empowered by God to interpret their meaning. His interpretations were correct: the baker was hanged, and the cupbearer was released from prison and restored to his previous position. Joseph's parting words to the cupbearer: "When all goes well with you, remember me and show me kindness; mention me to Pharaoh and get me out of this prison." Genesis 40 concludes with the terse statement, "The chief cupbearer, however, did not remember Joseph; he forgot him."

Two long years passed. When Pharaoh had not one but two very troubling dreams that no one could help him interpret, the reinstated cupbearer belatedly remembered Joseph's skilled interpretations. After Pharaoh's magicians and wise men proved woefully inadequate at dream exegesis, the cupbearer sheepishly approached the king with a fumbling apology: "Today I am reminded of my shortcomings … there's this guy I knew back in prison…." Again Joseph had every reason to wallow in bitterness. He had every reason to stonewall both the cupbearer and the king. Yet when he was sent for, he told Pharaoh the meaning of the dream: seven years of plenty would be followed by seven years of famine in the land of Egypt.

Out of gratitude, Pharaoh hired Joseph on the spot, giving him his signet ring (as a symbol of his authority), as well as a new name and an Egyptian wife, Asenath. An unforeseen "twist of fate" - perhaps more accurately referred to as "divine providence" - suddenly launches Joseph's life into an entirely new direction. Joseph's job was to store up grain for the devastating famine to come. After seven years, the famine indeed hit, and Joseph served as the administrator of the grain stores he had prepared.

While Joseph was distributing grain in Egypt, Jacob and his sons were suffering from famine in Canaan. Their once bountiful life as a family had deteriorated and they began to lay awake at night with guilt robbing them of sleep. Was God punishing them for their cruelty to their brother Joseph, and their lies to their father? They had no grain. They had no food to support their families and flocks. Their future looked bleak.

Jacob sent his sons to beg for grain from Pharaoh's stores. The brothers were brought before Joseph, who recognized them, though they did not recognize him. As they bowed before him, Joseph remembered his first dreams, when their sheaves of wheat bowed before his. He spoke harshly, accusing them of coming to spy out the weakness of the kingdom, and finally offered to test them. One of them could go back home to fetch their youngest brother — who was Joseph's full brother, Benjamin. The others would remain confined in Egypt.

Father Jacob refused to let his beloved Benjamin go to Egypt. But the famine continued, and the family stores withered away to almost nothing. Finally, the day came when they had no grain. Jacob realized there were no other options. He was distraught, but had to agree to send Benjamin, laden with gifts for the "man in Egypt." When his brothers arrived, Joseph invited them all to dine with him. The brothers were fearful of some kind of trick, but Joseph's steward (notably, a foreigner who unashamedly acknowledged the living God) reassured them that "your God, the God of your father", was behind it all (Gen 43:23). They feasted — but separately, as it was forbidden for Egyptians to eat with Hebrews. Joseph observed his family from a distance, particularly his little brother Benjamin, and was so deeply moved that he left and wept. The time to reveal his identity would be soon, but not quite yet. When the brothers prepared to depart, they were laden with sacks of grain, and all the money they had paid was also returned to them, concealed in their sacks without their knowledge. In addition, Joseph had his steward hide his own silver goblet in Benjamin's sack.

The brothers left bright and early in the morning. Shortly afterwards, Joseph told his steward to go after them. The brothers swore they had done nothing wrong. The bags were searched, and the goblet was found in Benjamin's bag. They returned to Egypt to beg for mercy and for their lives. Joseph offered to let them go — if Benjamin remained behind as his slave. This time, the brothers did the right thing. Judah pleaded for the life of Benjamin, telling Joseph their father would die if they left Benjamin behind. He offered himself for the freedom of Benjamin.

This righteous act was too much for Joseph. Can you imagine the flood of emotions he must have felt? He wanted this moment of utter transparency in private, alone with this crazy, messed-up family. He sent all the Egyptians away, and in a moment that must have knocked the very breath out of his brothers' lungs, he revealed the stunning truth: "I am your brother Joseph, the one you sold into Egypt. And now, do not be distressed and do not be angry with yourselves for selling me here, because *it was to save lives* that God sent me ahead of you. For two years now there has been famine in the land, and for the next five years there will be no plowing and reaping. But God sent me ahead of you to preserve for you a remnant on earth and to save your lives by a great deliverance. So then, *it was not you who sent me here, but God*. He made me father to Pharaoh, lord of his entire household and ruler of all Egypt."

Pause for a moment and consider your own story. If it is like most, the path has not always been pleasant and sunny. More likely, your story contains elements that you would just as soon forget. Some segments of the Christian community emphasize looking at one's sordid past and leaving it behind forever. We use language like "God plucked me out" or "lifted me," or "saved me from my past ways." But our full, unvarnished histories may be more valuable than we ever dared guess. Can we dare to ask ourselves whether the very aspects of our lives that are messy, embarrassing, and painful might just be the tools God has given us to reach toward others with great compassion and understanding?

You see, we can't have clarity about where God is sending us to save lives until we come to terms with our own storyline, with all of the situations, feelings, and faces we can remember. A memory bank can bring up the past for us in a nanosecond when we hear a song, smell a certain food cooking, or shiver from cold wind. The past is so full of God touches and shaping, things that do not easily fit into a "God plucked me out" testimony. So, maybe we choose to forget. But God overrides our forgetting efforts with a story that rises and falls at His will as He sends us into the future to save lives.

Our own messy family story holds a mother lode of clues for how and where God may choose to move through our seemingly ordinary - or extraordinarily dysfunctional - lives. Joseph, speaking with newfound clarity, declares: "It was God who designed this trail of events that led me to where I am right now."

Dare to imagine your life story as a tool, crafted by God in His infinite wisdom to accomplish amazing things. "To this you were called, because Christ suffered for you, leaving you an example, that you should follow in his steps." (I Peter 2:21)

40

God sent me to a soldier

My father was a World War II vet who shipped on the USS Prairie. He was always young looking for his age, but he was significantly older than my friends' dads. So, when I see an old World War II vet in a parade or just sitting on a bench, mustering all the dignity he deserves in his old feeble age, I feel right at home walking up to him and saying, "Thank you for your service, sir." To me, they are never strange aliens in funny old clothes with mean grimaces. They are my fathers. God sent me this father; I did not choose him. And as this World War II generation has almost died out, the question of where these veterans will spend eternity is on my mind — because God sent me to a soldier.

My family history and my personal story are exactly the things that enable me to minister in a very particular way. As I speak with people across the country, I urge people to look attentively and thoughtfully at their own stories.

A few years ago, I was doing an evangelism seminar in the Northeast. A wonderful group of Christians gathered, mostly professionals in their 50s and 60s. They had been in the church for most of their lives. I have an exercise I go through with the participants asking them to revisit the stories of their lives. The challenge is always to provide a safe setting for people to do the hard work of remembering their unique stories — events long forgotten, people lost in the back of their minds, experiences suppressed and hidden deep within the soul. I asked the group to take 25 minutes to write down "the story of your life."

At the end of the allotted time I began by asking, "Can someone tell me the story of before you were born?" One man answered, "My grandmother was a Christian who always had hymns playing in her home." The next said, "I was baptized when I was eight days old." A little disappointed at their safe, sanitized answers, I asked about the first five years of life, hoping to open the door a little wider. One lady said she remembered her Sunday school teacher and the church dress her mom always dressed her in. Another spoke about singing "Happy Birthday" to Jesus on Christmas morning.

I was beginning to feel annoyed — and I know I don't hide it well. So I said, "I need to apologize to you; I think I've set you up." I wanted to deflect the annoyance onto myself, as the group looked at me with growing distrust. Now I took a chance and just dove into what I hoped was the deep end of the pool. I turned to the lady to my right, made eye contact, and said, "Can you tell me about the real story of your life?" There was silence for a long awkward moment, and then some tears. And then harder tears, and she said, "I will not." Idiot that I am, I couldn't leave it alone, so I ventured right in where smarter fools fear to go. My eyes held hers as I asked, "Why?" She burst out in anger and hurt, "My husband was an elder in this church and he recently divorced me." Wow. I was taken aback and deeply moved at the same time.

Then something special happened. This dear lady turned out to be the kindling needed to start the fire going. Out came a procession of cancers, divorces, drunken fathers or grandfathers; the runaway children, the years of silence between siblings, the stories of people dying too soon and too young. There were the cries of the orphan, the stories of special needs children, the secret desire to play the saxophone, the lyrics of lost, hidden love, like an Elvis Presley song.

I always give the following instruction in these seminars: "If a crime or wrongful sexual act was committed against you, you might just use the code, 'for your eyes only.'" So later that day, after I had asked these dear saints to write out their life stories on paper, I saw sheets with the code written: "For your eyes only." After the session, a number of people came up to me and said, "Thank you, Al." Lost memories had been retrieved, and events that were too big, too complicated or painful to process when they had happened, had put them on a new course of remembering and honoring their life stories…a course that might take days or years to unfold.

We in the Christian community may have a "tone problem", though probably not an intentional one. We may have a bit of a superiority complex as we communicate the truth propositions of our faith and how they square with life's key questions. How can we shift our tone from a "king talking to a peasant" to "one beggar asking another beggar for bread"? The bridge is there: *it is the real story of our lives.* Is our redemption proposal worth anything if it can't be applied to our own lives first? We need the Christian world to tell the pain-strewn, ongoing story of our own broken roads without any nice, clean conclusions. You see, the Christian is a beggar too, only we have forgotten our story. Perhaps we have gotten disconnected from our own stories because we feel that we have been saved - called out of our pasts never to return - because the way forward is full of light and new opportunity.

But we don't know where we are being sent until we know where we have come from. What is your real story?? Can you remember? Is there a theological assumption or a character trait that has prevented you from going back? Way back. Back to your grandparents, back to the stories that were hidden or hushed up at family gatherings? To a single mom, a racecar family, a Down's syndrome child, a bankruptcy, or lonely, prison-like toil in a factory? God sent Elvis a stillborn brother, and He has sent the events in your life as well.

Remember them. Recognize their impact. Trace out the silent finger of God in your past. Learn your Joseph story.

Chapter 5

The Mother of All Questions

I'm going in circles
Need direction first degree
I'm going in circles
Help me through my misery
I can see the light through this blindfold
Mine is a story that's still untold
Take my hand and lead the way . . .
Going in circles and I want to be free
Things ain't going the way they used to be
Run outta gas and you know it ain't fair
Don't want this circle, I ain't going nowhere...

Robbin Moses Kapsalis
Vintage #18

Growing up, I was one of five siblings — three boys and two girls. The three brothers lived in the basement. I bunked with my younger brother Jeff; Bob, being three years older and the firstborn, got his own room. Bob was secure in himself. Being a great tennis player and leader of the pack in family order suited him well, and he rose to the responsibility. When his chosen position as grand marshal of our family circus became tiring, he could always retreat into his solitary bedroom hideaway.

Late evening or early morning — well, actually, any moment of opportunity that presented itself — there would be espionage-like raids between Bob's bedroom and mine. (My little brother, Jeff, had a blood pact with Bob, so an enviable peace held between them.) For some reason, Bob loved reptiles and he happened to have a strange, fear-inspiring guest living in his room. It was a four-foot iguana that he had raised from an eight-inch mail-order creature. I am not making this up. He would feed the beast a head of lettuce or, if money got tight, dog food as a substitute. The dogs never knew. Perhaps I was jealous of this stupid reptile that seemed to have such a nice bedroom to himself with an endless supply of food and an owner who caught him large bugs for breakfast.

One of the stealth night raids I made on Bob's room was to reconfigure all the volume control knobs on the soundboard of his stereo system. Bob had an impressive stereo system as well as an enviable record collection, the kind of collection that first-borns save, organize, and file neatly. And so the plan was hatched, and potential witnesses were busy with other things. I made my way into Bob's room — oh, the delight of all the little levers and knobs! I laughed as I changed them, thinking of the earsplitting sound that would result.

What happened next was something I had never imagined in my ten-year-old reptilian brain. You see, Bob had placed his beloved iguana as an armored security guard, draped over the stereo in his room. I had only seen that stupid lizard in statue-like poses, and even wondered in the back of my mind if he was truly alive or newly stuffed. But the iguana was fully alive now, and he did what iguanas are born to do: wind up and whip the enemy with their tails, which make up over half their body length. His tail hit me on the neck and continued around my neck and down the front of my chest. Oh, the sting of death! I couldn't yell or cry, let alone accuse anyone or even devise a plot to kill the iguana. His tiny brain won the battle that day.

And then I heard my mother's voice: "Din-nerrr!" Uh-oh. When she called, you came right away. As five hungry children knew, when food was served, a quick arrival to the table was expected. I grabbed a turtleneck from my drawer and put it on before I ran to dinner. I knew that right after the dinner prayer Mom's CT-scan vision would check over each child to detect any injuries, weapons, unusual smirks, or guilty, suspicious stillness. That laser beam would scan the four other kids in one minute and would then settle on me. To be honest, I earned that laser-beam stare with stories I would rather not put in this book. I always sat next to my father, whose right arm could inflict swift punishment, and he liked it that way. Mom asked the mother question: "Allan, why are you wearing a turtleneck?" It was midsummer and of course swelteringly hot. Manipulating Mother's guilt was always the best ploy, so I said there were no clean clothes in my drawers. Across the table, my brother Bob began to look at me closely. This wasn't going to end well.

Mom said, "Al, look at Allan's neck under the turtleneck." I didn't dare stop Dad's probe with those WWII machinist's hands.

"Oh, my goodness, boy, where did you get that welt?" Dad kept pulling at my shirt, exposing the entire length of the lash around my neck and down my chest. It was raised a good quarter-inch off my skin. My brother Bob's eyebrows were now shooting to the sky, and a smile was spreading across his smug firstborn face. I answered in a quiet monotone, "I ran into a branch in the woods." The answer seemed to take the heat off, as everyone knew that the woods were my first home and my bed my second. Mom asked if it hurt, and I said, "Not much." As for my brother, life was good and getting better. My lie might have diverted the parents' suspicion, but he knew better. He won that round, hands down.

We had tapioca pudding for dessert that night, but I passed on it, under the knowing look of Bob's well-deserved V-day celebration. The welt lasted for three months.

I had been sure that the turtleneck would hide the evidence of my crime, even from the examination of a loving, engaged mother. But a mother can't stop trying to keep her son safe, and I knew that my parents would be engaged. Parents are filled with love, and that love involves the hard work of truly caring about their children even in the most difficult moments. They continually seek us out: as toddlers, children, teens, and even as adults.

Discovering us where we hide is one of the greatest things a parent can do for their child. God's care for us, too, is evident as He patiently watches us hide, calls our name, and waits for our answer. He wants to find us again and again, even when we think we're hiding so well from Him. In one of the greatest scenes in Scripture our heavenly Father describes our own birth and creation, almost like an awestruck young dad gazing through the nursery window at his firstborn. Listen carefully to the Father's words in Genesis 1:

> Then God said, "Let us make mankind in our image, in
> our likeness, so that they may rule over the fish in the
> sea and the birds in the sky, over the livestock and
> all the wild animals, and over all the creatures that move

along the ground. So God created mankind in his own
image, in the image of God he created them; male
and female he created them.

God created two thinking, creating, celebrating, introspective,
self-checking beings, who would have the ability to communicate
with their Creator and hear His voice. God made man a conscious
being, something that has fascinated scholars in many academic
disciplines. The number of books, lectures, and graduate degrees that
have focused on our state of being conscious is simply amazing. God
has endowed human beings with a vibrant inner thought world. He
declared the entirety of creation "good", in the deepest and truest
sense of that word. He delighted in walking, communing, and simply
being present with His creation.

Then something happened. Evil arrived in God's created
paradise.

Now, the serpent was more crafty than any of the wild
animals the Lord God had made. He said to the woman,
"Did God really say, 'You must not eat from any tree in
the garden'?"
The woman said to the serpent, "We may eat fruit from the
trees in the garden, but God did say, 'You must not eat
fruit from the tree that is in the middle of the garden,
and you must not touch it, or you will die.'"
"You will not certainly die," the serpent said to the
woman. "For God knows that when you eat from it, your
eyes will be opened, and you will be like God,
knowing good and evil."

The scriptures tell a tragic story about how the angel Lucifer
sought to become God, fell away from God in outright rebellion, and
then turned his attention to mankind — the brand-new children in
whom God delighted.

Adam and Eve, of course, took the bait so enticingly proffered by
Satan. Pondering the rewards, they made an informed decision that
would affect all of mankind. Lured by the serpent with the delusion of
becoming God, they took the fruit from the tree and ate it, exactly the
thing God had forbidden. The serpent's damage was done. In spiritual
terms, he wound up and whipped his tail, lashing Adam's neck around

48

the back and down the front of his chest. This cataclysmic welt would linger as long as people walked the earth.

Then, on the cusp of this desperate moment, we hear something in the quiet of the garden. We hear the voice of the Father.

> Then the man and his wife heard the sound of the Lord God as he was walking in the garden in the cool of the day, and they hid from the Lord God among the trees of the garden. But the Lord God called to the man, *"Where are you?"*

If I was directing this movie, God would surely have spoken away all the sheltering trees, leaving Adam and Eve bare in His presence, and He would do what the gods of the movies do — shout in anger, exuding rage and balls of fire. However, God does not do this; he does not even say, "I told you so." Instead, he begins with a question, perhaps the mother of all questions: *"Where are you?"* It was a question that recognized Adam's endowed ability to answer. It was a question that offered him dignity. The Father knew where Adam and Eve were hiding; yet he offered them the opportunity to answer and to hear their own words.

Adam spoke honestly and said he was afraid. He *knew* something traumatic had happened to the world in which he was living. He also answered honestly, and with shame, that he was naked. See this moment in your mind: this first living image of God, in the presence of his Maker, fully accountable for what he had just done.

God listened to Adam's fears, answers, and his feeble attempt at justification. And then he unleashed the weight of Adam's blatant disobedience:

Pain...
Cursed is the ground...
Thorns and thistles...
Sweat...
Return to dust.

This weight rests on the shoulders of every human soul. It is an unbearable weight, and each soul sags under it. And every precious soul made in the image of God *lives under the curse.*

The human soul needs to tell the story of the Fall, to hear its own anguished cry, *and to be heard.* When I would sit in the blues bar and start a conversation with a person near me, I would programmatically ask, "How are you?"

And without fail would come out — what hurts.

You can often hear someone burst out and say, "What is wrong with this world?" whenever wars or gruesome crimes are reported, or maybe a hurricane has wreaked havoc. The soul is speaking from the surface of the image of God, insisting that these things should not be so. Or the soul speaks out from its own torments when it is seeking a sex change, or something to end its life, or drugs, alcohol, or a fourth divorce. The soul is crying out, "Something is wrong here!" Day after day we echo the ancient question of the soul on our cell phones, in our jobs, and in our marriages: *"Where am I?"* I believe that the unchurched souls all around us are asking this question, throwing out less-than-satisfying answers and hiding behind bushes, fig leaves, turtlenecks. I believe many are secretly pondering this question all the time.

Yet when we talk to people, we often address them with little awareness of the questions swirling within them. We assume that the human mind is simple, like the reptilian brain, caught up in finding the next meal or job, a girl or a smartphone app. But perhaps there is far more going on there. Could it be that, just as God speaks the mother of all questions in the Scripture, all humans carry this question around in their souls? Could it be that the soul wrestles, ponders, imagines, and hopes far more than is evident on the surface, as each of us asks, *"Where am I?"*

Blues, country, classical, rock, rap music . . . so much of it is the story of Adam hearing God's footsteps and trying to hide. Of lamenting the brokenness of every area of life and seeking a way out. Victor Hugo says, "Music expresses that which cannot be said and on which it is impossible to be silent." (Hugo's Works: William Shakespeare, Part I, Book II, Chapter IV) Music channels the cry of our soul. We can't seem to fix our damaged, fragmented lives or our fractured world. Maybe we are hearing the voice of death itself. Suddenly we ask ourselves, *"Where am I?"*

Listen to the question within your own soul. Wrestle with it.

Then listen for that question, unexpressed but present, in those around you.

Listen - wait for it to surface … and come alongside.

Chapter 6

The Birth Line

I always hoped the steps I took
Would lead me towards you
Now I understand
That you arrived on time
By angles and degrees only when the day was right.

Emily Morrison, I Bless the Day We Met

When I came out of my layman "camouflage," and my friends all knew my line of work, I could always count on Tracy to deliver a shot across the bow any time I walked into the blues bar. Tracy was amused and delighted that I had ventured out of my religious closet into her world of bikers, blues, and beer. She could be mean when she wanted to, and I was occasionally on the receiving end of it, but mostly it was just ribbing. She would say things like, "You're not going to convert me today!" or, "Is Jim Bakker still in jail for stealing all that money from those little old ladies?" She wanted me to know that all the tricks Christians play on the unsuspecting were well within her radar. Her weekly run-ins with me were a kind of hobby; they never reached the point where I would stop coming, or wished she would go away. She would wait for me to walk in the bar. She would walk all the way across the room, touch my shoulder, and post her "No Trespassing" sign on any words of mine that might pull her into the religious world.

She would cuss at me and then sort of apologize, always in jest. And of course, she would talk loud enough for everyone else to hear, because she knew she spoke for them too; she enjoyed her growing and appreciative audience.

Something was up with Tracy. Maybe my "Spidey-sense" was tingling, or maybe I just saw her as a challenge, someone to outlast or even outwit, maybe land a reply that would stop her mocking altogether. Yet Tracy was someone that inched into my mind each week; I began looking forward to her signals of strength and comfort in her non-belief — in God, the church, or Jim Bakker. Maybe there's another option here . . . maybe Tracy was being brought alive by God Himself. Not in a loud, hands- thrown-in-the-air, "Hallelujah, I've seen the Light" kind of way — but something much smaller. A tiny conception planted by God himself in her heart.

Is a baby conscious of itself at conception? No. Is everything already working at conception that will make the baby physically viable? Again, no. But life has started, and it will grow and develop in a hidden place until the right time, when birth will take place. I began to imagine Tracy as a host to God's Holy Spirit making His mysterious way into her. Maybe a pregnancy was in motion in her soul. When Tracy would protest my presence or my words, my thought was, perhaps she protests too much. I'm happy to say that she is now a regular attendee in our blues church community. We talk often, and she even whispers prayer requests to me, and she still taunts me about not EVER becoming a convert!

Memphis Slim sings a song about a mean watchdog that is surprisingly friendly to a man who is having an affair with the man's wife. I think of that mean watchdog wagging his tail when I think of Tracy's inner watchdog beginning to let down his guard, waiting and wanting to hear a prayer that will mean something to her. This is how God begins to shift us from our unsustainable loves to His ever-present love. The lover that the soul is always craving is God Himself. When his Holy Spirit is working, the watchdog begins to be charmed. The conception of faith is already taking place in the hidden places of the heart, and this takes time.

My own spiritual pregnancy

My own story has its seeds in the life of my mother.

When I was an infant, my 15-year-old mother stood in line at the Baltimore welfare office. Deep in her young heart she felt angry, humiliated, placed in a strange world with strange stares in a process that stole her dignity. Off in the corner was a black-and-white TV - fuzzy, but the only distraction available. It broadcast a Billy Graham crusade. Yet another voice telling her what was wrong with her. But then something sparked, and her inner watchdog started to let down his guard and be charmed by this gentle voice. She accepted the call to receive Jesus. She felt something burn alive inside her. Dignity could be found in the act of asking Jesus into her life. What did she have to lose?

Mom's arms holding her little ones had something to do with the unfolding of this story. Her delicate young arms were holding me for a reason. These tiny ones who had come into her world in such an imperfect, unplanned way needed her nurture, her protection. She wanted so much more for her children than she had experienced as a child.

So I was raised in an atmosphere of belief, however dysfunctional my home.

Flash forward to when I was 10. The police arrived at our door on a cold winter morning to inform us that my dad had been in a terrible accident. He had driven to work in his VW bug, like he did every morning. This particular morning he negotiated a curve as he always did, but in the blinding glare of the morning winter sun he failed to see the stopped car sitting on the curve. He hit that car going 65 mph. We were told that the broken bones were too many to count; the steering wheel smashed through his rib cage; his head went through the window. The little car was crumpled like an aluminum foil ball you would throw in the trash. I remember, at his hospital bedside, the doctor told us to say goodbye. Those words could not come to me, even though I probably tried. Instead, the prayer cut loose. "God, if You're real, save my dad!"

He lived.

I figure that my spiritual pregnancy was maybe in its ninth month.

The Birth Line

But by the grace of God I am what I am, and His grace

to me was not without effect. No, I worked harder than all of them — yet not I, but the grace of God that was with me.   *1 Corinthians 15: 10*

When I think about my story, it is easy to forget all that personal history. Instead, I am tempted to credit my salvation to the sermon or experience that immediately preceded my conversion to Christ. Cornelius Plantinga writes something similar: "When I contemplate my own conversion experience, I am tempted to hang the time of enlightenment to God's truths upon the sermon of the preacher who immediately preceded the time when I committed my life to Christ."

The pastor who gave that sermon has always been a bit of a hero in my mind, a large man who expressed large emotions as he talked about heaven and hell. At the end of his message, he issued a passionate invitation to anyone who would like to accept Jesus as his or her personal Savior. I had not yet made the decision and so, at the age of 13, I asked Jesus into my heart. But in reality, God was at work in my life long before that point. If my life were arranged along the Birth Line, it would show a long and careful journey towards Christ. A very real time of "pregnancy" took place through the warp and woof of my life.

So far, we've been discussing the work of God to shape and influence us through life's experiences and encounters. We've talked about the mother of all questions, *"Where are you?"* But how do we come, personally, to put our trust in Jesus Christ?

This is *our* Birth Line, our own faith journey.

It is not always an easy topic to discuss with others. Where do we begin? Why do we suffer communication paralysis when it comes to sharing our faith or conversion experience of becoming a Christian? Why does it sometimes sound like a neat, pre-written script? I suspect that the message we give others doesn't really square with our own experience of becoming a Christian. We know that it took much more than a few minutes or hours for Jesus to come into our own lives. It may be that the Christian community has paid too much attention to the moment of conversion and too little attention to the period of time that leads up to that moment.

Perhaps we can start by asking ourselves this question:

"Where did I first experience the Lord calling me to Himself?"

If we stop to take a closer look at our own process of coming to faith, we can bring that knowledge to bear upon our witness to others.

Recognizing this subtle, often indiscernible spiritual development in our own lives will revolutionize the way we minister. It will help us immensely as we learn to respect God's schedule as it applies to the lives of those around us.

This concept was first presented to me through the instruction of Reverend Steve Smallman, the former pastor of McLean Presbyterian Church in Virginia. Steve is a respected friend and mentor who taught me a great deal about being a pastor and disciple. He introduced me to the concept of "the spiritual birth line." Steve suggests that when Jesus talked about being born again (John 3:1-12), he intended for his audience to think about physical birth. Steve developed this approach to illustrate the two "births" in the life of a believer.

Physical birth:
Conception – Pregnancy – Delivery – Growth

Spiritual birth:
Life begins – Regeneration – Conversion – Sanctification

The physical birth line begins not at the time of visible birth, but rather at the time of conception. Similarly, the spiritual child is conceived well before the actual public event of professing faith in Christ! In fact, the spiritual birth line of the conversion experience begins not with the moment of confessing Jesus as our Lord but with the moment of physical conception. The implanted seed leads up to physical birth. And similarly, the implanted spiritual seed leads over time to spiritual birth. Archibald Alexander, writing in 1841 in Thoughts on Religious Experience (part of a 20-volume work), observes: "The implantation of spiritual life in a soul dead in sin is an event the consequences of which will never end. When you plant an acorn, and it grows, you do not expect to see maturity; much less the ends of the majestic oak, which will expand its boughs and strike deeply into the earth its roots" (Alexander, p. 22). The true power of this birth line lies in helping us understand that God deals with us through a process of time, events, circumstances, people, and a multitude of other influences that all make piercing spiritual impressions upon our hearts and minds. Jesus understood that this process was occurring. In Scripture, we see again and again that Jesus attended to the current life needs of the people around him; he showed his awareness of the events that took place in their private lives. Think of the poignant stories of Nicodemus, the woman at the well, and the calling of each of His disciples.

As with the physical conception of a child, the time following that germination of life is filled with intimate nurturing moments and events. It is God who begins the process of spiritual life, and it is God who nurtures the seed of the Gospel with many methods and messengers until it comes time for that visible, tangible event: the time of the new birth.

While the power of God is indeed able to regenerate the sinful hearts of mankind in a millisecond of time, His normal way of dealing with His children uses many molding influences. People are moved, drawn, and enlivened by God in innumerable ways. But during the process of conversion, God's movement is sometimes hidden within events that seem quite normal. An old friend turned up; you came upon a book; a new job obligated you to reexamine your goals; an unexpected illness caused you to face your own mortality.

Consider the many people that God has woven into your life throughout your time here on earth. Consider the grandparents, or even the great-grandparents, who impacted your spiritual development, whether you personally knew them or not. Perhaps an early impression of your grandparents has always been just a few thoughts away from your conscious thinking. Consider the impact of the spiritual journey that your parents have taken, and the spiritual issues that they directly or indirectly have wrestled with, regardless of whether they were Christians. All the words you overheard or that were unconsciously registered in your mind — they all amount to something! God begins very early in our life to pose God-sized questions, and has created within us a sincere search for answers.

In the same way that an obstetrician takes a stethoscope to detect the first fluttering heartbeats of an unborn child, perhaps we can begin to learn to listen for those first clues of spiritual conception. To do so, we must be quiet... attuned... attentive.

Evangelism 101

When I was 12, we attended a little Bible church down the road. Pastor Denny was a follower of the Jack Hyles school of Bible teaching. I was at the beginning of my faith journey, wide-eyed and naive. Our method of evangelism was to knock on a door in a neighborhood and wait for someone to answer. We received guidance in grooming, smiling, and courage. The method was to say these words to that person: "If you died today, would you go to Heaven or Hell?"

I remember the house. The cement steps were crooked, the screen was torn, leaves were spilling over the gutters. The man was old; I guessed, in my seasoned 12 years of life, that he was likely 50. He opened the door, and I said, "If you died today, would you go to Heaven or Hell?" There was a pause. The man looked me in the eyes and said, "Son, I don't know the answer to your question, but if you don't get off my porch you're gonna find out." I sort of sensed that something hadn't gone very well, but I wasn't sure exactly what. I told my story at the round-up time and was praised for courage. In His time and space, God blesses and chooses not to bless some things, including our best efforts.

Another method was to visit bars at night — the ones with rusty pickup trucks with gun racks and no paving in the parking lot. At around 12 or 13 years old, I was invited along on this night mission of "special ops" forces. I'm not sure my parents really knew the whole picture — but, hey, it was a church event and Allan was invited. The method was to go to the bar around 11 pm and begin to preach through a bullhorn, out in the dirt parking lot. I gathered that the men in that bar didn't respect or appreciate our courage and our pure motive of fixing their souls. A bearded man wearing camouflage walked out of the bar, wobbling a bit, held up a gun, and said, "Get the **** out of here — now!!!" We ran back to our station wagons and reflected, out loud, "Such God-haters!"

God can bless our ridiculous efforts. Even after we butcher the Gospel and His glory, still God will choose to bless our frail, self-absorbed methods.

Pastor Denny asked me if I wanted to become a bus captain. I said okay. My territory would be a trailer park in Taneytown, Md. Every Saturday I would go visit the park and tell people that a bus would be there on Sunday morning to pick up their children and take them to church. Men would answer the trailer door in their "wife beater" shirts and boxers, hear the words, "I'll take your children," and they would answer, "The kids will be ready." The trailers were full of cigarette smoke, fried food smells, barking dogs, and matted shag carpet. They always said yes; they didn't ask me my name and serial number or do a background check on me. As I visited these children, I was exposed to shocking humanity. The kids were usually ready Sunday morning at 8 a.m. The old bus was loud enough to signal our arrival. Many of the kids dressed themselves as their parents or stepparents slept off hangovers from the night before. The kids called me Pastor Al; I was thirteen years old.

This was the beginning of my calling. I began to love those children. I remember stepping over big, snoring, passed-out men, to reach my arms out to a waiting four-year-old. Each week a different child was allowed to sit with me on the front seat of the bus. If you came to church, you got a free McDonald's hamburger, and I would buy the fries myself with the money I had earned working at local farms. If you got converted and came forward at the altar call, you got a free, brand new Bible, presented in front of everyone on the bus. Someone got saved every week, and we had the Bible presentation for each child.

In my self-involved middle-class educated mind, it's easy now to look down on these people, as well as the church that reached out to them. But even here God can work and move. God uses what He uses, in His time and space, without our approval. This flawed, silly, pay-you-to-get saved model was my avenue of call into the ministry at age 13. I loved those children and they loved me. I still miss them.

Effectual calling

"Effectual calling is the work of God's Spirit, whereby: Convincing us of our sin and misery, Enlightening our minds in the knowledge of Christ, and Renewing our wills, He doth persuade and enable us to embrace Jesus Christ, freely offered to us in the Gospel."
Westminster Shorter Catechism, #31

I remember being asked to visit a dying man, the father of a member of my congregation. He had consistently rejected anything that had to do with his personal relationship with God. He had resisted the efforts of his family and even the most articulate and dedicated ministers that God had brought into his life - and there seemed to have been quite a number of them. Yet one thing became very clear to me:

this man was not ignorant about spiritual issues. His eyes said, "I'm ready to talk," while his body told me, "I'm almost done here." His voice was broken and humble.

Whenever I came to see him, we would talk about construction work. He was a residential home contractor, and I had been involved in that line of work for much of my life. We would talk about how the methods of residential construction had changed, and I was impressed with the analytical mind that God had given this man. At each visit we would talk about carpentry and construction, and I would always end by holding his hand and praying for him. I remember well the feel of his leathery, calloused grip against the surface of my smooth preacher hands. Each time, tears came to his eyes and we exchanged a warm good-bye. At about the fifth visit, this man looked at me and told me that he needed to get ready to meet God. We shared some Scripture together and then, in a childlike way, he said the sinner's prayer. God's grace defined this moment that had eternal consequences.

Reflecting on this scene causes us to ask the questions: How did that conversion experience take place? Did this man first encounter God with my visits? Was that analytical mind of his stuck in neutral concerning spiritual issues for all the years preceding our meeting at this hospital bed? The answer is emphatically, NO! God had him on a spiritual birth line, and I was privileged to be present at the moment of delivery. God had used many, many people, events, circumstances, and thought processes to bring him to the point of new birth.

Though an old man, he was a baby in Christ after a very long pregnancy. Praise the Lord for all those who labored in prayer over this man's soul years before I even met him. Furthermore, if we look closely at this dear man's conversion experience we can detect a pattern that we see, time and time again in the lives of God's children. It is a pattern of subtlety and nuance, unique to each individual person. Who was most important in the long pregnancy period? Certainly it could not have taken place without the implanted seed of truth. After the seed was planted, who was the most important messenger or cultivator along the way? We are tempted to conclude that I must have been more able or articulate than all who had gone before me. But by God's grace I simply arrived at that moment when he was ready to listen with new ears.

Again, Archibald Alexander provides a colorful picture of this conversion process:

"It may be justly and scripturally compared to a growing crop: after the seed is sown it vegetates, we know not how, and then it receives daily the sun's influence, and from time to time refreshing showers; but about the time of harvest, after a long drought, there comes a plentiful shower, by means of which, nutriment is afforded for the formation of the full corn in the ear. No one will dispute the importance and efficacy of this last shower in maturing the grain; but had there been no cultivation and no showers long before, this had never produced any effect."

Conversion is a *process*. God used all of the people and circumstances of this man's life, including his impending death, to bring him to a point of personal commitment to Christ. I was the individual who appeared at the time of harvest. Others had labored long and hard to share the Gospel and had been an example to him for many, many years! The vital point to consider is this: preceding the event of spiritual birth there is a long pregnancy period, where God uses many voices and vehicles to call His children to a point of embracing Jesus as their Savior.

Spiritual "midwife"

Steve Smallman reminds us that "we are not called to be salesmen for Jesus, trying to 'close the deal' no matter what it takes; we are called to be spiritual midwives, available and ready to help with the birth." If we can grasp the whole Biblical teaching behind this lesson on the birth line, many doorways into becoming a more effective evangelist and disciple will begin to appear.

I believe the "confrontational dialogue" paradigm is radically altered when we apply the truths of the birth line. We begin to be freed from the tensions and the quandary of how to relate to people who don't yet believe. We can breathe, listen, and be present with people, rather than wondering when we can interject our scripted truth. We begin to recognize our own presumptuous attitudes. God has each of us on a schedule and a birth line. The point at which people commit their lives to Jesus is most often the conclusion of a long string of divine events.

If we can see that God has planned and initiated the pregnancy and all the influences that sustain that growing spiritual life, our method and philosophy of sharing our faith will change. Our role moves from authorizing the germination of the spiritual life to being a midwife or encourager to an event that is beyond our control. The style of evangelical Christianity that is constantly pushing people toward salvation to get them "converted" — manipulating them with music, repeated invitations, or a sort of sales routine — is an ugly deformity of Christian practice that results in bad doctrine. This does not mean that we avoid confronting people with the truth, but that truth telling must always be combined with a listening, respectful ear.

God does use our warm and persuasive presentation of the Gospel, but on His timing and not ours. Seeing that our ministry to others is carried out in the context of a "birth line" can release us to a model of ministry that places value on the pregnancy period as well as on the time of birth. The challenge of revealing the "secrets of the kingdom" to people with closed eyes and calloused hearts is that it is usually a slow and invisible process. People who become followers of Jesus and stay committed to Him often move toward Christian belief in the same way an embryo moves toward full development: cell by multiplying cell.

The birthing experience

When a child is born, it is usually in the context of a mother struggling with great effort to deliver the baby. "Push" takes on a whole new meaning here. Once born, the child senses the dramatic change of environment and will react with crying that brings a soulful smile to everyone's face in the delivery room. Spiritual labor and delivery can be a similar process. The moment surrounding the time of conversion can be full of effort and emotionally charged — understandably, considering the significance of the spiritual birth! The conversion experience can often be remembered in detail, clearly placed on the map and the calendar. Whenever someone is asked about her spiritual life, there is comfort in being able to share the specific day and place where she trusted in Jesus as her Savior.

All spiritual births are not the same. Many of God's children enter the kingdom of God with little or no emotion associated with this eternal event. The reality of the new birth is not valid because we know a specific date, but it is shown in a dynamic faith that trusts wholly in Jesus Christ. God works in many ways as the hearts of mankind are kneaded and nurtured by the work of His Spirit. Those who have placed their trust in Jesus, regardless of the circumstances surrounding their birth into the kingdom, are truly the sons and daughters of God!

Knowing that God works in people's lives through many different experiences and on many different schedules releases the Christian to speak into this gestation period in countless ways. The journey to Christ is a process, not just an event.

One of our most common mistakes is to try to share everything all at once. We wait for an opportunity to share our faith with a friend or acquaintance, and when the opportunity comes, we unload the whole message and even call for a decision. Few people are ready for that; more often the attempt results in polarization rather than in faith. Jesus taught that coming to faith is a process (John 4:38). It is not always harvest time, but it is always time for something: planting, cultivating, watering, or harvesting. It can be a relief to realize that we are only part of a process. The salvation of an acquaintance, friend, or family member does not rest on our shoulders alone.

God has orchestrated our lives so that we meet different kinds of people who have an authentic relationship with Him. Perhaps we encounter God through their prayers at dinnertime, or the Christmas cards that reveal that Christ means something real to them. People who become part of our life's crises, accomplishments, and questions can be used in a powerful way to nurture a spiritual appetite in our souls! If we dare to take time and reflect upon the pregnancy period of our own conversion experiences, we begin to recognize a profound web of people, circumstances and encounters. If God has worked through others' lives to reach us, the question we must now ask is: How is He working through my life to reach other people?

God can use us in a myriad of ways to nurture, cultivate, and ripen the implanted seed of truth in the heart of the people He has placed in our lives. One of the men in a class I lead, often reticent about speaking in front of others, asked if he could share a recent incident that changed his way of thinking. Gary has an office in downtown Washington, DC. He is in the advertising business. Every week, if not every day, a certain homeless man would approach him and ask him for money or try to engage him in conversation. Gary described his normal attitude as "rather fed up with this guy," and he would often walk a block or two out of his way just to avoid him. This man never seemed to change, and instead of trying to improve himself he was always asking for something!

During the week following our class discussion of the spiritual birth line, the same scenario unfolded. Gary was walking to his office, only to be approached by this homeless man. As Gary described this incident, he related how his view of this man was transformed. No longer was this man a nuisance. Gary realized that God had this homeless man on a different birth line schedule than his own. This man had been brought into Gary's life as an opportunity for ministry! The thoughts, seeds of kindness, and truth that he could share with this homeless man might contribute to the progress of his birth line. Gary said, "A light went on. I could see a new role I could play in this man's life!"

If we look carefully at the process of our own conversion experience, we gain a radically new perspective on our witness to others. The perception that others are "in process" has revolutionized the way I think about people, and has released me to minister to them where they are. There is no single meaningful moment for this ministry: the time of spiritual birth is not the "only" meaningful encounter with others. God can use us in myriad ways to nurture, cultivate, and ripen the implanted seed of truth in the hearts of the people He has placed in our lives — a process of cultivation that may be beyond our own ability to fully detect.

Two Stories

When I conduct evangelism seminars at churches around the country, one of the things I do is ask participants to reflect on, and then write down, their spiritual birthline. As people reflect on both the obvious and subtle influences that have shaped their spiritual journey, they often see with more clarity the work of God's Spirit in their lives. I share two of these stories below. Just as each pregnancy is unique, no two birth-lines are exactly the same. The Psalmist, in

Psalm 139, says with wonder, "You knit me together in my mother's womb". So too our spiritual lives are woven and spun with great precision and purpose by our heavenly Father. Reflect on your own story as you read the narratives below.

Nelson's conversion experience

I am 42 years old and have attended church since I was a little child. I have lived in Northern Virginia almost all my life. I am the second of two children born to an older couple. My father spent time working for the federal government. My mother was a wife and mother, never working outside of the home. We were raised in the Episcopal Church (my mother's denomination). Between my birth and graduation from high school, my family moved only once.

My father's family was from Maryland. My grandfather was born in Germany, and my grandmother was born in the USA. My father's family was from Lutheran background, and my grandmother and uncle were very involved with their church.

My mother was from Georgia and met my father while he attended Georgia Tech. My mother trained at a secretarial school and was raised by her grandmother because her mother died when she was only one week old. My mother was not a well person, being born with petit-mal, a form of epilepsy. My mother was raised Episcopal and did not know a day she didn't hold the Lord as her Savior.

My parents were married 12 years before my brother was born, and therefore he was the jewel in their crown. I came later, and arrived seven weeks early. I never truly felt loved. My brother was artistic, and was coddled and protected by my mother. I was viewed as being independent, responsible, and resourceful and therefore I could take care of myself.

My mother spent many years in and out of the hospital. Through it all her faith never wavered, never weakened. I remember, near the end of her life, an episode that struck me as odd. I overheard my mother talking with my father about the fact that she was dying, and she said "I don't care what will happen to me. I know I am going home. I just wish I could spend more time with you."

There was never any question of Dad remarrying. There had been only one woman for him, and with her he weathered all kinds of storms. My mother died when I was 16. She had an experience on her deathbed that my father was witness to and which we believe was repeated 22 years later with my brother's death. Near death, she began to talk quietly to someone. My father kneeled down to hear what she was saying. She put her hand on his head and said, "See, God, this is my husband, please take care of him." She smiled and then slipped into a coma.

I went away to college five days after I graduated from high school. It was the first time that I was on my own, the first time I was responsible for no one but myself. It was a rocky road. I dropped out for a year and returned home to work. But mainly I was typical of the era. From the age of 17 to 24, I was a drug addict. Someone once asked me if I'm being a little harsh on myself, but God knows that I'm being honest when I describe myself this way.

When I was 21, my brother became a Christian. He did many things wrong from the start, especially alienating my father by writing him off as an unbeliever. I saw the hurt it caused and wanted no part of a religion that did that to someone. Through all this, I began to read a Bible he gave me and went line by line through John. I would write him these long letters filled with questions, but he never wrote back. Whenever I returned home I would go to church with him to be supportive. There I met people who were truly interested in me. They never preached, never judged; they loved me. It was this love that broke through to the person who was starving inside.

But still I remained in my life and lifestyle. I had this notion that I had to get "clean" before I could turn to Christ to "get right with God." I knew there was more to life than what I was feeling inside. There was emptiness inside me that drugs, alcohol, sex, or whatever thrill would not fill.

By my senior year I lived off campus, and due to the interruption in my education, I was older than most seniors (at 24). I do remember one psalm sticking in my mind about how I felt. It is Psalm 32. To this day in my Bible, I have written next to this psalm, "my witness psalm of my conversion." The verses that kept haunting me were these: "For day and night your hand was heavy upon me." My strength was sapped . . . but it was like running on a treadmill. I couldn't get the notion out of my mind that someone was catching up to me, but I was afraid to look back and see who it was.

One day in August 1975, I returned to school to get ready for the fall term. I spent five hours alone in the car with my thoughts, returning after spending time with my family and with some families from my brother's church. This persistent feeling that I was being followed and watched kept creeping up on me. Finally I pulled up to the apartment I lived in, occupied by drug users and dealers. All my resolve dissolved just by walking into the lobby. By the time I was in the apartment I shared with my girlfriend, I was back at step one: high and disappointed with my weak resolve and myself.

I remember walking into the bathroom and looking at myself in the mirror. But this time I wasn't alone. I now saw whose hand was heavy upon me, as it says in Psalm 32. Behind me was Jesus showing me His mirror — what He saw when He looked in it at me. It was an image I couldn't handle. I had been trying to get myself right before I met Him where He was — and in turn He told me that He would meet me where I was. It wasn't that I had to stop the sin before I came to Him, but I had to acknowledge my sin. He removed the heavy burden of my sin and through Him I had the strength to change paths and walk with Him.

As I weaned myself from drugs and alcohol, everyone I had lived with and partied with became suspicious. My friends wanted no part of the new me. What finally broke me from the old life was actually graduating and returning home to live. I became involved in my brother's church and settled into a new life. Once in awhile the old life would call up or visit. Each time the Lord would use these times to show me that light truly has nothing in common with darkness.

Richard's conversion experience

I'm a 31-year-old freelance writer and an ordained Baptist minister and seminary professor. Essentially, I don't recall a time when I didn't believe in the facts of Jesus' earthly existence. My parents were both Christians, strong and committed in the faith, but my father in particular was aware that each person has to come to an understanding of Christ on his own.

During high school, I was clearly searching for spiritual grounding that I did not get in the Baptist Church that I attended as a youth. I studied most of the world's major religions, particularly eastern religions. I did extensive reading in the scriptures of Hinduism and Buddhism, and although I never adopted them officially, a number of my friends later told me that they fully expected such a conversion. During this period I still read the Bible from time to time and maintained an interest in Christianity.

66

After graduating from high school, I lost interest in religion for a time. Eventually I ended up back in California, where I attended Humboldt State University and commuted home to the Bay area on most weekends. It was at this point that I began a very intense reexamination of Christianity. I experienced a profound depression, and this in turn led to an examination of my life as a whole. One day I came into class and it was a lecture on the American theologian Jonathan Edwards. The only way I can describe my reaction to the lectures on Edwards is that I was stunned. I was simply enchanted with the brilliance of Edwards's mind and the clarity of his theology. The professor taught us that Edwards was a Calvinist, and I thought that if Jonathan Edwards was a Calvinist, then I needed to reexamine my opinion of Calvin.

I went to the college library and checked out John Calvin's Institutes of the Christian Religion. I checked Calvin's assertions against the Biblical verses that he quoted, and I was amazed to find that Calvinism was simply another name for the theology of the Bible. From there, I decided that a rereading of the Bible was in order. The method that I used was to simply read the text and ignore everything that I had been taught about it, simply letting God speak to me through the text. God used the experience to change my life. I came away from that reading as a convinced Christian and a convinced Calvinist.

The spiritual birth-lines of Nelson and of Richard are just two examples of the working of the Holy Spirit. Each story is unique - both common and remarkable at the same time. But the truly beautiful thing is this: God's unseen hand is in each story, and he uses regular people like you and me to be a part of it.

Chapter 7

The Image of God is Speaking

Bare feet stepping on glass
We break along life's paths
Our fear and loss, we bring it all to you
Soul-breather, making all things new
You're making all things new

We come in pieces
We come in fragments
We come discolored
To the foot of the cross
Our Maker sees us
All that we have been
Bonds us together
The Image of God

Christa Wells & Nicole Witt, "Image of God"

I went to Las Vegas with my buddy Chris. It was January of 2013; he had a builder's conference to go to and needed some company. I had never envisioned myself visiting Las Vegas; just the thought of "sin city" had kept it off my must-see list. But here was Chris with a plane ticket for me and a place to stay. I said what any man raised in a religious fundamentalist home would say: Sure, I'm in!

I had a cartoon image of what the city would look like, smell like and act like at 6 in the morning. But the cartoons in my head didn't really capture the strange ethos of Las Vegas. All the escaping suburban inmates stretching their freedom for one last night before returning to their prison cells: the work cubicle, the responsibilities, the traffic, the middle-age crisis, and all the rest of "back home." The swirling mass of food vendors under gyrating fluorescent colors and pulsing neon signs, the opulence and noise of the casinos, and the herds of people heading from slot machine to gaming table while staring at their smartphones — the racket quickly overwhelmed most of my senses.

Something churned deep within me, a sort of soul-nausea. I tried to talk myself through it. Just chill. I'm OK. I can handle an altered reality. But my internal churning continued. Something in this place was very wrong for my inner being. I was in the wrong place and watching the wrong people, still trying to stay unaffected by the humanity all around me. Since I don't gamble, I had figured it would be safe to just stand by and watch the people who do, telling myself, "I'll never be as stupid as these people." But worse, not everyone I saw was here to play gaming tables and slot machines. Outside the casino, every ten feet or so, someone holding a sign looked me in the eyes: "Out of work. Please help," "Hungry," "My kids thank you." Or maybe, "Take a picture with Elvis." And then there were the ones who couldn't hold up a sign even if they wanted to.

The immense size of these casinos boggled the mind. I couldn't see the beginning or the end. Dinging noises and blinking signs were everywhere. To simply walk through these places you had to somehow turn down the sensors and microphones built into your body. It was a loud, bright, windowless village. You could gamble, eat, sleep, get a pedicure, smoke, dance all night, get Starbucks coffee and every other kind of beverage as well. You could be vacationing or working, do your taxes or meditate, and never leave these walls.

And many, apparently, had never left. The elderly people in walkers and wheelchairs at the slot machines smacked me in my self-righteousness. I was smugly looking down on the drunks and out-of-control middle-aged men going wild, but these people who were barely able to walk jolted me. My eyes got watery. One dear man could not get from his slot machine to the bathroom — so he did what he had to do, right there where he was, and people just moved away from him as if it happened all the time. It didn't seem to faze anyone, and a staff member eventually showed up and seemed to know the routine.

Here I was, 52 years old, and I was hoping my mother would never find out I came here. I kept walking and I came to the gambling tables for blackjack and all the other games, with a dealer at the head of each table. At one table, a beautiful woman in a tight, low-cut dress was masterfully playing the men, while the men were playing the odds against the dealer and each other. Laughter switched to anger and back again ten times a minute. Everyone was using everyone one else, and everyone was going along with the game.

Did I mention the cameras, the uniformed security and plainclothes security, patrolling the floors? I wondered what they were thinking as they strolled through and around this rabble of humanity. Then I noticed all the men at the poker tables wearing sunglasses. Of course. The casino lights were laser bright; migraine triggers, no doubt. Or maybe they wore sunglasses to be cool. No, someone informed me, the sunglasses are to hide the giveaway glances that gamblers can't hide, so other gamblers can't guess the card strength they're holding. Bluffing, retreating, cockiness, disappointment, excitement — these are body language tools that seasoned gamblers can control and feign. I was impressed by how these guys could stay so still watching through their asphalt-thick sunglasses and putting on good theatre for spectators like me. I stood quietly by my friend Chris, nonchalantly pretending I kind of belonged there.

All our scars

Whether or not you are wearing sunglasses, you still must live in the image of God. The image of God is the eternal DNA, the double helix structure, housed in every human soul. We can work hard at our profile and image on the outside. But God created the inside with a voice, mind, and compass for navigating the human experience. The image of God is pressed upon the surface of the soul like a tire track in soft red clay. The questions, whispers, the sense of justice are intrinsic to mankind. Behind the sunglasses at the gaming table sits a soul who is thinking, fragile, seeking, confused, and questioning.

There's more behind those sunglasses. There always is. As I write this, I'm sitting near the beach in southwest Florida. Every body shape and gender, mostly over the age of 79, is sunbathing. I remember, growing up as a fundamentalist teen, that the teaching on mixed bathing was a significant point in all spring sermons — no swimming at the beach or the pool where girls would show up. Even if the sermon started with Moses and the burning bush, somehow mixed bathing was threaded in as a sin. I remember raising my hand in youth group, as a snarky 14-year-old, and asking if mixed bathing was OK in the family bathroom but not the beach. But sitting on the beach in Florida, I noticed something more serious. For the first time, I noticed the scars on people's bodies. My biker buddies in the blues bar back home had scars on their faces and arms, but they were wearing their black leather jackets and worn jeans. Their scars looked cool and manly.

On the beach the scars were exposed. They told stories of knee and hip replacements, heart operations, lung and kidney problems. One guy had a PICC line taped to his chest for his chemo later that week. No body part had been spared: necks, backs, or limbs. Missing pieces, like parts of noses, ears, faces, or divots in the skin. Colostomy bags. Never mind the plastic surgery. The scars tell a story. But where do the scar owners go to tell their story of the hurts and terrors to which those scars point?

In all the surveys I have done and questions I have posed interacting with the unchurched, I hear one loud, unmistakable question that comes back at me in unguarded moments. "If your God is so great, why is my life so hard?" For most people, the idea of sin is not an answer. They wonder: why is this God (or Being) picking on me? Ok, I'm bad, but is there an end in sight? People have emotional as well as physical scars, too many to count or even process. They try to soothe themselves with a great airbrush job to hide the inner stitch marks that won't go away. The mother who birthed a stillborn son, the teen with a drunk father who died 10 years ago but still lives in his head; these are suffering people who have learned to hide their scars. When cancer shows up, or another personal tragedy erupts, the soul cries out, "Really??" The elephant in the room, as it relates to the soul, is suffering.

There's something else here. The church as a whole hasn't come to terms with suffering. As we wail and grind along in our own pain scenarios, we too question God's goodness. The unchurched watch church-folks as they struggle with their own personal pain, more closely than we might imagine. They hear our reasoning and they detect our sugar coating, our clean apologetics. They pick up on our dualism: happy, happy in public, but sad and tormented in secret. Suffering is damn hard, this genius path used by God to awaken and call His dear children into the kingdom. Yes, God harnesses even the blackness of death to bring about Life. And I think the non-churched want to be welcomed into our suffering. Please hear me: I am not saying suffering in any form is easy, or that it feels right, or that we should act like angels who were just given their first set of wings.

As I sit and write this sentence, I'm pretty obviously scarred myself, two weeks out from a second jaw surgery. I shattered my jaw on a fishing trip, in a freak fall. Love and support came at me from all directions, not just from my church. My blues buddies have all called and visited, and my Jewish surgeon and my dentist have called, visited, and texted me. I am simply overwhelmed by all the love and care, and their empathy has helped me to recover and renew my sense of wellbeing. Frankly, I couldn't keep them away. At one of my blues bars I have made a number of African-American friends. The black ladies would soothe me with their words and questions, leaning in to touch and hug me. They let me in as one of their own; it was a felt gift that I can't explain. Sure, Pastor Al helps, prays and holds other people in distress —but Pastor Al also has scars. I asked my blues buddies to pray for me, and they did.

Does God hear the prayers of those yet to be Christians? Can He even hear their voices? Does He care, or does He turn away and say, "I never knew you?" Those prayers, given from people who don't claim to be church people or Christians, changed my life. We bonded over prayers, and their lives began to change as they were asked to pray for Pastor Al. One of my blues friends said, "I don't know how to pray." The words "Yeah, you do" came out of my mouth, and he nodded with a smile. You see, the soul is made to talk; it's made to talk to God. When we talk, yell, accuse, or even curse God, the person deep inside us communicates with someone. The image of God seeks out God in all of us. As Christians, we have been so focused on the "front narrative" — what people say in our debates — that we haven't heard the "back narrative," the one where people secretly wish it's all true….or perhaps dread that it might be.

Sometimes we discover how the image of God speaks and lives inside of us as we reflect on the brokenness of our earthly parents and on our own mortality. Who doesn't know that moment when you see your dad or mom looking back at your own face from the bathroom mirror? We perceive, both for better and worse, their profound influence in our lives, our unshakeable connection to them, and our deep, deep longing to be loved and accepted by them. When we lose our parents, we are left as orphans crying out for someone to hear us, to love us. It's a moment for the *Image Maker* to meet the *Image Child*. Our cry is deep because we are crying for something deeper - deeper even than the loss of our earthly parent.

When my father died at 87 years old I asked out loud, "God, how could you take him so soon?" I slept by his bed the last four nights of his life, in hospice. I whispered each day, "Dad, it's ok, you can go." I knew he'd be worrying about mom, worrying if there was gas in her car and the windows were closed, and if his secret switch to the water heater was turned on. Then I told him that I had to go home. He had been in a coma for four long days. I drove away, and as I got to the fourth traffic light the nurse called me. "Your father has passed, Mr. Dayhoff." I loved those nurses; they helped dad die well, and they gave him some dignity, too. Then it came: tears like I can't ever remember crying. I sobbed like a dog run over in the middle of the road, half alive, half dead and dying hard. I couldn't see the road any more. I was so angry and hurt and sad my chest hurt. The wrenching pain of loss was deep...deeper than I can convey in mere words.

There are two reasons why funerals are so somber. It is partly over the tragic loss of the deceased lying silently in the casket. And it is partly over the thought, "When is *my* turn coming to be the guy lying up front?" I believe we have lost the awareness that the souls of men and women are alive with spiritual questions, fears and secret yearnings: "Maybe there is a God who made me, designed my path, and waits somewhere for me?"

This morning, at a cigar shop, I asked a guy in sunglasses what he thought about church people. He laughed and said, "They live in a fairy tale. They inherit a set of thoughts from their parents, and then try to prove to everyone else they are right — because deep down they fear their religion may not be true." He laughed, and I laughed too. He puffed on his cigar, and I puffed on my cigar. Then he pivoted his sunglasses to the top of his head and he said, "My dad died two weeks ago; I hope he made it in."

Maybe it was the cigar that clarified the image of God.

My study on the beach wasn't yet finished. I started seeing all the tattoos around me with new eyes. Did these marks on the outside of the body give clues about the inside? I have always wanted a tattoo, but by now my skin is a little less, shall we say, elastic. There were tattoos from World War II, like anchors and other things that I couldn't make out because the skin was not exactly smooth or stationary. On the under-60 group there were skulls and bones and dripping blood, scenes out of a horror carnival booth. It's as if they were saying, "I'm familiar with death and evil, and I can send signals to strangers that I'm not afraid. I have inner strength; I'm living with the power of darkness and it can't stop me — for now."

Then there were the tattoos of people's faces, with dates. These people had died, and the people they left behind had written their names and memories over their own hearts: fathers, brothers, sisters, and, yes, babies. I go where other fools fear to go, so I asked one sunbaked lady, "What does your tattoo mean?" She looked at me and said, "My daughter died in a car crash; that's her." She moved her top over to show me.

"Thanks for telling me," I said.

"Thanks for asking." Then she was gone, and so was I.

Hearing the Image of God

Five Big Questions

What questions are we using to listen to the image of God in the people around us? As I have interviewed hundreds of people and had my evangelism students do the same, I have zeroed in on five simple questions that seem to draw out the image of God. I want to share with you my five God-sized questions, and I want you to be the judge of them. Here they are:

1) Where do you believe the world came from?
2) What do you believe about God?
3) What do you believe about Jesus Christ?
4) What do you believe about life after death?
5) If you could ask God one question, what would it be?

Let me invite you to evaluate these questions not only in your seminary class, around your breakfast table, or in your book study. Let me invite you to try them out on the street, around the Thanksgiving table, on a plane, in a biker's bar, with your young children. Your job may be hard: *you must only listen*. And maybe your listening can break into hearing. Hearing the image of God, hearing the stories of pain, the sounds of an orphan, hearing the seeking side and the haunting words that long for hope. One thing I have discovered is that the longer someone talks, the more they talk themselves *toward* God, not away from Him. Sometimes the "slip" doesn't come until the very last question; other times, it bleeds out in every other word.

I hope you will ask these questions with no plan to answer them, but only to listen, to see if by listening you can hear someone's heartbeat. Hear the image of God revealed in them. People want to be discovered — not *"truthed"*.

Let me take a risk here. It's not so hard for most people to believe that someone or something created the world. Its complexity, beauty, and natural mechanisms meet us every waking moment, and maybe every sleeping moment too. But many people, even though they suspect that the world is no accident, prefer to hold their cards close. Why should they let us into their secret thoughts, anyway? Would we respect the room of their secret thoughts, or would we drive a dump truck full of our "truths" into that special room? People are very savvy about the chessboard moves of the church and especially about its evangelizing of their unchurched souls. They have cottoned on to our scripts and our serious role- playing with our practice sparring partners.

Maybe the sign that our listening finally breaks into hearing is when we can truly feel the words we speak — as in, "I am so sorry." At that point, someone has dared to give us a chance to really hear personal sorrows and pains, trusting that we won't just revert to our own script. This is the beginning of a faith relationship with many delightful chapters ahead. Yes, the gospel gives us hope beyond and around our sorrows; but pain is real and must be heard. Heard by you and me as we listen...not to change, not to judge, but to *hear*. The church today seems to think that so many people are just pagans who never consider God — never even wonder about the three human questions all souls must ask: "Where did I come from?" "Why am I here?" "What happens after death?" The truth is, everyone comes to the point that is the end of themselves and the beginning of God, even if it comes at the moment of physical death.

May I give you a window into one of these dialogues? The following is a sketch of my talk with Bill…

Bill is a stable man in his fifties, well educated and not afraid of me, or my faith-talk. His worldview could be summed up this way: "What's good for you is great, what's good for me is great, and that's what makes the world go 'round." He agreed to take my 5-question survey when I told him that my only role was to listen to him and see if I could hear what he was saying. It put him in the driver's seat. I wasn't setting him up, and he respected that and believed it to be true.

Question #1
Where do you believe the world came from?
When I first asked the question, Bill went through an elaborate scientific explanation: "Evolution and science holds the only real answer out there." He went into genetics, the vastness of time, the discoveries in Africa, and even such things as Carbon-14 dating. Bill said that there is only one good answer, and that's evolution and the survival of the fittest. I wrote all this down and asked if he had anything else to say.

He began to speak about Darwin, the Galapagos Islands, and the Smithsonian Museum of Natural History in DC. He then talked about Stephen Hawking, who said, "God not only plays dice; He also sometimes throws the dice where they cannot be seen." Hmm, I thought. Then Bill said, "Even if there is only one possible unified theory, it is just a set of rules and equations. What is it that breathes fire into the equations and makes a universe for them to describe?" He told me, "There is no heaven or afterlife for broken-down computers; that is a fairy story for people afraid of the dark." I said to Bill, "This is very valuable, got anything else?" He said, "No, that's it, Al. What's the next question?" But before I could present Question #2, Bill commented, "But you know, where the first matter came from is a crazy puzzle for the mind, isn't it, Al?"

"Sure is, Bill," I said. I had a promise to keep: I was only listening.

Question #2

What do you believe about God?

"Wow," Bill said, "you don't play around, do you?" He launched into some questions of his own. "What makes you think there is a God? Does he speak from a cloud, or jump out when you're in the forest or something? Ha-ha. Does he look like George Burns or Morgan Freeman? You know all the wars of the world seem to be about whose God is bigger, you know? And by the way, you Christians aren't exempt from killing people and starting fights because people don't believe." Bill paused, and then he asked the real question. "Where is God, as my wife is now in her second bout with cancer? Al, why would God do that to such a good woman and mother? Go ask your God that question, Al, and let me know what he says, would you? I'm done with this question, Al."

Question #3
What do you believe about Jesus Christ?

"Hmm. You know, my mom was a Christian, and she would pray around the table at dinner. My dad thought it was nuts, but he didn't mind either. He said he couldn't close his eyes at prayer in case someone stole his dinner. Ha-ha. Mom wore a cross around her neck; it was gold and we buried her in it. Jesus likely lived and was real, but all those miracles like healing the blind and sick, well, it's a stretch. You believe that stuff, Al? Oh, that's right, you can't say anything. Smart man. All I know is, a big fuss is made at Christmas and Easter, he must be real to somebody. Crosses kind of creep me out, because bad things happened on them, right?"

"Anything else Bill?"

"Yeah. How can this Jesus help my sick wife?"

Question #4
What do you believe about life after death?

"Well," he paused. "My mom's in heaven. She believed it and lived it. I can't imagine her not getting in. My dad and me, that's another story."

"Bill, can I ask an unfair question?"

"Sure, why stop now?"

"If there is a heaven, would you want your kids to be there with your mom?"

Long pause. "Is this almost over, Al?"

"No Bill, I have questions that will keep us here to next Monday, ha-ha!"

"I don't have a good answer for you, Al. I'm not gonna cry."

"Oops, too late, Bill."

"I hate you, Al." Bill's body language was suddenly less confident, shrinking as if a hidden sorrow had been pinched.

"I know you do, and that's why we're friends, Bill, ha-ha. We are almost done; let's get through this last question, Bill."

Question #5
If you could ask God one question, what would it be?

"God, are you *real*? How can I come to believe in something I can't see? If you are real, why are things so hard here on earth? Why did all those people die in 9/11 in such a horrible way?"

"Anything else Bill?"

"No. Maybe — how's my mom doing?"

This interview with Bill shows that people are alive in the image of God. Martin Luther King, Jr. said it so poignantly in his well-known speech, "I Have A Dream":

> The whole concept of the Imago Dei...the 'Image of God', is the idea that all men have something within them that God injected....This gives him a uniqueness, it gives him worth, it gives him dignity.
> And we must never forget this...there are no gradations in the Image of God. Every man from a treble white to a bass black is significant on God's keyboard, precisely because every man is made in the Image of God.

An active search is going on in the secret places of their minds and hearts. The unchurched may wear sunglasses, hiding their souls from untrusted speakers. Inside, they may be wishing that someone would ask them about that scar that cannot tan, and how it came to be. Or hoping someone will read the cryptic messages in their tattoos.

But the Judeo-Christian ethic that undergirds much of what we think and say is unfamiliar territory to most people. Yes, they may have grown up with a grandma, an aunt, a neighbor or friend who exhibited Christian faith, but their perception of a coherent, believable Christian worldview is non-existent. More than that, it's irrelevant.

So we must go to them. And here lies the gift I was given in going to the blues bar. I stumbled upon the bar because I wanted to hide there. But the people in the bar *needed* me to be there, *where they are*.

I have learned to love my bar, and the people in it. In all honesty, their friendship and kindness make me cry. They want to know what I'm doing, where I'm traveling, what book I might be working on. I am brought back to the point over and over as I sit in the bar: it's a listening room. I listen to the blues songs channel the stories and emotion of my heart and of theirs. But it's more. As I listen I get amazing rewards. Trust builds stitch by stitch with each minute of simple attentive listening. The longer people talk, the more they talk themselves toward God. The most active listener is often the person talking...trying on different answers right in front of me. Trust builds as I listen quietly, being present without judgment. Do I feel as though my job is to be part of getting this band of hitchhikers to the other side? Yes. You see, my dear friends are so much like the thief on the cross who turned to Jesus and said "Umm . . . could you remember me when you get to the other side?" It's not my job to fix sexual dysfunction, alcoholism, anger, mental illness (perhaps 20% of the people in the bar), loneliness, or theological errors in the way people think. It's my job, I suspect, in my own broken way to say: "Dear friend, I want to see you on the other side. You ready?" But I only do so when they ask.

Oh, and they do.

Chapter 8

The Resurrection of Sabbath

The soul that loves God has its rest in God and in God alone. In all the paths that men walk in in the world, they do not attain peace until they draw nigh to hope in God.

St. Isaac the Syrian, Homily 56, 89

During my years as a pastor my Sunday mornings were full of highs and lows. Most Sundays I enjoyed preaching; the text meant something to my own soul, and sometimes I would finally "get" the text in the midst of my sermon. But whenever someone said, "Great sermon, Pastor, but...", I knew that this might be the hidden signal of a difficult coffee meeting ahead.

Following each week's service I would enter into at least 20 conversations about people's stories and their hurts. I appreciated the sacred space into which people invited me, and I sensed God's pleasure when I sought to understand the difficulties, or even chaos, of their lives. A marriage on the rocks, a bad medical result, a child suspended, a pink slip, a crisis of faith — difficult circumstances that always prompted some version of the question: "Is the Bible true and the way to go?"

There were also the hard Sundays of conflicts over whose job it should be to fix a leaking roof, or teach the adult education classes, or pay the mortgage, or fix the sound system. And I got used to the debater who would wait for the sermon to end and then somehow block my path to the back door. On other Sundays I was not Reformed enough, or I told stories that went on too long, or I didn't make the gospel plain enough. The hard part was, my critics were usually right.

The children were always a delight. I loved the little boy who called me "Aster Pal" instead of Pastor Al. I loved doing children's sermons, giving one simple, easy-to-swallow message, and I knew that it was the adults who would benefit the most — including me.

So being a pastor has always been a calling in my life and one I have delighted in, though at times (I confess) I have wondered whether something else was waiting around the corner. But on the dawning of each Monday morning, I was always pretty tired, pushing down feelings of depression, anger, and a desire to be completely and utterly alone.

My usual solution was to load my 100-pound chocolate lab into the truck (with 400,000 crazy trip miles already on it) and head to the Potomac River. Harley never cared about my sermons, or about what I was wearing, or about my state of mind, or whether I was a Christian, or how tired I was. Just the sight or sound of my arrival sent his body into leaping delight. His tail was a rubber whip that you treated with respect. The possibility that I might throw him a ball evoked uncontrollable dancing — and all the better if I would send that ball 300 feet into the flood rapids of the Potomac.

Once, coming back from speaking in Philadelphia, I pulled into a spot along the Susquehanna River, near Route 95.

Harley was in my truck; he travels everywhere with me, as long as it doesn't get too hot. I parked at a remote section of the river and opened the back hatch, and Harley leaped out as if this was his last adventure in this life. Picking up on his enthusiasm, I grabbed the tennis racket and hit the rubber ball as hard and far as I could, into the river.

Then I noticed a couple of things. The river was flood stage, and the January temperature was about 27 degrees. As big as he was, I saw Harley get swept away immediately in the fast water. I didn't panic, but the thought crossed my mind that this might be the time he didn't come back to me. And how would I explain this to all the Harley fans in my life?

I waited a long 35 minutes as sadness came over me. I thought about making a second cup of coffee on the propane stove. And then I saw the tiny brown dot, way off in the distance, running straight at me. It was Harley; I could not mistake his locomotion. But as he got closer I saw he had become an ice sculpture in motion — each hair was now encased in frozen slivers of water. As he got closer it began to crack, the ice shedding off his fur. And — he had the ball. Harley placed that round reward at my feet and then stared intently in my face to signal, "Let's do it again!" And we did! I threw that ball five more times before leaving the river. Harley slept all the way home, preparing for the next outing. Clearly, Harley got the Sabbath.

Exodus 20:8-11 reads:

> Remember the Sabbath day, to keep it holy. Six days you shall labor, and do all your work, but the seventh day is a Sabbath to the Lord your God. On it you shall not do any work, you, or your son, or your daughter, your male servant, or your female servant, or your livestock, or the sojourner who is within your gates. For in six days the Lord made heaven and earth, the sea, and all that is in them, and rested on the seventh day. Therefore the Lord blessed the Sabbath day and made it holy.

This sacred Sabbath has become a lost delight even though it is a desperately needed source of recovery for our souls. We never rest our bodies and souls from the insecurities, loneliness, and labors that seem to imprison them. Sabbath can replace these burdens with a time of simple play that can make our spirits breathe and our hearts sing.

Observation and remembrance of Sabbath is one of the Ten Commandments. Implicit in the definition of Sabbath is "re-creation," or the recreation of the mind and soul. It's a day of worship: seeing God's worth and letting that knowledge feed your own particular soul in a real, knowable, and distinctive way. What was my particular Sabbath? For any pastor, the church is the place of work rather than of rest or recreation, and it also has its own kinds of stress. The organ music in high church worship settings, for example, creates a tension inside of me: I neither like it nor feel God's presence in that music. So, each Monday, I found myself retreating again and again to the river with Harley for a few hours, never able to get enough — of what? Enough Sabbath to rest; enough play to fill my soul with the wonder of God's presence in creation.

God walks in His garden with us

Genesis 3 gives us insights into the ways of God with His children. It reads, "Then the man and his wife heard the sound of the Lord God, as he was walking in the garden in the cool of the day." No doubt God enjoyed walking in the beautiful garden he had spoken into existence. But He especially loved walking with Adam and Eve. We can let our imaginations wander a bit and ask: What did that walk look like? I think God's creation gives us hints into just how God longs to walk with us.

Did you ever see a grandpa walking with his five-year-old granddaughter as she chatters away, holding his two fat fingers and delighting in the safety of this big old joke-telling man she calls "Poppy"? Ever see a teenager walk his brand new, scent-crazed puppy in a park in the springtime? Ever see a mother duck cross the road, with her fast-footed brood of seven small ducklings behind her? Ever see a professor, hands clasped behind his back, as he walks with a freshman student on campus, listening to questions he's heard 500 times, while offering fresh ears? Ever see God our Father, in the garden with Adam and Eve, listening as He walks to the sound of toucans and monkeys calling in the treetops? Have you ever pictured yourself walking in God's presence as you live in the particular thing that delights your soul?

Perhaps Sabbath is truly one of the keys to fruitful ministry in our next season of evangelism. We are not able to be truly present with other people when we haven't allowed God the time to fill the void in our own soul. St. Basil the Great said, "As it is impossible to verbally describe the sweetness of honey to one who has never tasted honey, so the goodness of God cannot be clearly communicated by way of teaching, if we ourselves are not able to penetrate into the goodness of the Lord by our own experience." *(Conversations on the Psalms, 29.)* I believe that Sabbath rest is the care the evangelist so desperately needs as he reaches out to others. Our souls are tired and lonely, and they long for a walk with God alone.

People today are surrounded by noise of all kinds. They have their senses, their souls, and their psyches assaulted constantly as they seek to navigate the noise of the social media revolution. Psychologists are now developing terms for people who have lost touch with what is real, who have an impaired ability to separate the virtual from the actual.

What do vacation planners advertise in their commercials? Quiet places for minds and souls. Car manufacturers describe the car's interior as a safety zone shutting out noise and pollution as you are serenaded by high definition stereo in gridlock traffic. Spas are inventing ways to quiet the noise of our world and our hearts. In this noisy world, noisy souls are looking for someone quiet they can talk with. Can the evangelist be that quiet person?

Centuries ago, the monastic movement understood the problem of noise and the soul's need for solitude and quiet. Theirs is the art of listening and hearing. The broader Christian church has dismissed the monastic way because it can't be quantified; and, yes, it was a broken system, like every other system run by broken men. But there is value and benefit that we desperately need today. C.S. Lewis wisely observes, "We live, in fact, in a world starved for solitude, silence, and private: and therefore starved for meditation and true friendship." (*The Weight of Glory*)

I think it is safe to say that we have become a noise-filled people; our interior lives are often chaotic and messy. We are all about doing, memorizing, systematizing, and planning, but not walking with God and simply being in His mysterious, fulfilling presence. How can we listen to others if we are not listened to? How can our *listening* becoming *hearing* if we don't feel that God is hearing the whispers and the fragile fears of our own souls? How can we hear the noise that is so threatening for others if the background noise in our own life is not quieted — with God — in Sabbath rest?

Could it be that sometimes, in our eagerness to share the good news of the gospel, we charge in uninvited with our rehearsed phrases or unwanted explanations? Could it be that the fears and defenses of our own souls crowd out the unspoken need of others to be heard? We feel guilty. We feel inadequate. We feel afraid. And so we have no quiet space within to which we can invite others. I believe that God delights in using a quiet soul, one that can simply be present with whoever is ready to come into the kingdom, whether sooner or later. And perhaps the way forward for our next generation of listening and hearing soul-winners is for us to resurrect for ourselves a precious Sabbath rest.

For many people, Sabbath has come to mean trying to keep yet another set of rules one day a week, rules that we often break and pretend we don't. That pretense can build up inside us like a scary ice dam on the Susquehanna in January. Maybe we should think of keeping Sabbath as an art form rather than a set of rules. It's up to each of us to learn how best to recreate ourselves and restore our own inner peace, to be equal to the difficult task we have set ourselves.

I've been thinking a lot about Sabbath rest lately due to a freak accident that actually prevented me from talking for about three weeks. I had been fishing for 12 hours on the Chesapeake Bay without thinking too much about taking care of myself. I became deeply dehydrated, and on the way home I began to vomit in the truck. My friend, who was driving, stopped at the side of the highway and I stepped outside. My last memory was telling myself, "Don't fall into traffic!" I hit the concrete face first and woke up in the ambulance with unbearable pain in my jaw: both hinges and my chin were broken.

Who would believe this story? Not the doctors, who wanted to know what really happened. Then I met my surgeon, a specialist named Dr. Z. His words, tone, and body language said clearly, "I am so sorry, Mr. Dayhoff, so sorry." His very human empathy gave me the energy to open myself to the journey that lay ahead, and his work inspired empathy in me as well. There was grace all around me. My soul was filled through empathic care from my wife, my loving blues buddies, and from my mom asking me to "describe the pain" as if she felt it herself. Their empathy elicited something deep within me — it enabled me to shift from focusing on my fear and guarding my manhood to being able to receive the well-chosen words and the tender care of those who are dear to me.

After the first surgery the swelling nearly closed off my ear canals completely. My jaw was wired shut and my ears were all but useless. I could watch what others were doing, and hear them if they shouted. I was closed for business. But my core became activated, my powers of observation increased. I found a great new joy in the nearness of my wife, who served me hand and foot, and in the empathy shown by Dr. Z. and all of my hugging, soup-making blues buddies; life had become a big, BIG joy. And my soul needed quiet to get there. What else had changed? Can I be honest? Maybe the best kind of evangelism I was capable of came in those difficult weeks:

God had wired my jaw shut! Wired-shut became my sanctuary; God was in it. I started *truly hearing*.

Another confession: I worried what jaw surgery would do to my face. Would it turn into a "no" face, a perpetual scowl? I could see my blues buddies staring at my face after they heard the gruesome details. Then Gary put his finger on it. "You know, Pastor Al, you might be left with a permanent smirk!" Inside I was mortified. Left with a smirk? I started to look at the faces around me — the "yes" faces, the "no" faces. Well, maybe this made some kind of sense. The pastor is the one with the smirk face. Could it be that my new jaw and face and mangled diction are building my empathy, giving me a clearer eye to discover the blues people that God has brought into my life?

Or maybe it's God's way of teaching me to listen. A second lengthy surgery has gifted me with a synthetic jaw socket; now every time I speak my ears pick up the squeak of the Teflon and titanium. It's a constant reminder: "Al, whenever you hear the squeak, don't talk, just listen."

Breaking one's jaw is probably not the best way to regain the Sabbath experience, but it was a powerful one for me. Being forced to listen and not talk, forced to depend on the love and the kindness of others. Feeling gratitude for the healing power of the body and for the care of a gifted surgeon. Having more time to reflect than I usually allow myself. However our Sabbath comes, it is a time for the core to be quieted, experiencing the presence of God and being fully welcomed into mystery. Our souls are noisy — in the Christian community just as everywhere else. When we stop tethering Sabbath rest to rules and regulations the Sabbath will radiate God's presence in immeasurable ways. And that presence will spill over into the lives of those around us.

Chapter 9

Where do we go from here?

Don't you have a saying, "It's still four months until harvest"? I tell you, open your eyes and look at the fields! They are ripe for harvest.

John 4:35

Well, you have gone with me on this crazy journey into my blues bar. I've given you some windows into my own broken story - a few of my own sorrows, joys, and discoveries. I've let you peer over my shoulder into the eyes and hearts of some of my blues friends. And I've invited you into your own journey; one in which I've asked you to look back and look within, so that you can move forward with more wisdom, sensitivity, and integrity.

The next question is: Where do we go from here?

Are you, like me, so moved by the beauty and power of the gospel that you long for others to experience the life-changing reality of God's grace?

I have found fields white for harvest in the most unlikely of places - a blues bar. What fields do you see surrounding you: in your neighborhood, your town, and your relationships? What is your "Joseph story" and where might God be sending you?

May I offer some closing thoughts, based not only on my own experience, but also on the experiences of many others with whom I have worked to continue exploring new avenues of evangelism?

Stop talking

One Sunday in the blues bar, I asked one of my new friends what he thought of church people. His answer was immediate: "If you would all just shut the h*** up you might learn something." Ouch. Another phrase I have grown accustomed to hearing is, "Today, nobody listens to anybody." People are just waiting their turn to jump into the conversation and present their side.

Parents who were about 22 years apart in age raised me. I love both of my parents, but as I remember it, each of them sort of talked in the direction of the other person, or maybe to someone else as if referring to the other person. They rarely talked directly to each other. One day it dawned on me that I was just like them. As we listen to someone else talking - particularly someone with whom we might potentially disagree - we are always framing a response ... a "yeah, but!" That "yeah, but" steals our hearing. It shuts down communication. It blocks empathy.

Our apologetics can be an excellent discipline. However, when we respond, "yeah, but," we are limited as to who we can reach. "Yeah, but" lives in a superiority complex, in the arrogance that comes with having too much knowledge and too little self-awareness of our own secret idols...idols of pride, of self-righteousness, of theological correctness.

Real empathy conveys a feeling of being cared for that goes beyond our particular point of view; it begins with a genuine interest in the other person's story. Not to rebut it. Not to edit the story to one that makes us more comfortable. But to truly hear the other person and hold their story with gentle respect. When someone in my evangelism seminar asks, "But Al, when do I speak back?" I answer: "When they ask you to" — and that might take six months or more.

A conversation is not ten or twenty minutes of talking in a doorway. It takes place over months and years as the relationship and faith discussion and "listening to hear" play out. We earn the right to speak through being quiet — soul-deep quiet, honest about our own struggle with suffering, and waiting to be asked our opinion. That is when we can begin to weave our own stories into the stories of others.

Evangelism: a passionate fishing expedition

I have shared with you my love of fishing. But I'm a rookie: I stand next to real fishermen and try to imitate them, and occasionally I get to take the rod when they have a fish and reel it in.

What I have learned from these real fishermen is their passion for everything involved in fishing. They love the smell of salt water, the sound of the surf, the whirr of the 225HP motor at full throttle. They have 48 different lures, and they can catch their own bait in the surf. They love sharpening their filet knives and getting a sunburn from the water. I recently saw one angler catch a sea trout, slowly feel the side of the fish's body and ponder the artwork of his neon colors. It was a magic moment as he then released him back for another day. He whispered something to the fish: I think he said, "See you next year, buddy." Evangelism might best be lived in a fishing boat, pondering the head winds, the type of fish at hand, the fickleness of a certain species, like the pull of a fighting bluefish caught in New England in the fall.

Let's take sheer delight in the moment, in the never-to-be-replicated setting — and in the beautiful, unique soul in front of us. From so many years of pastoring, I realize that the ever-present question below the surface of every person is always simply, "Does Pastor Al like me?"

Every time he sees me, my buddy Chuck says, "Al, you're not gonna convert me today." Honestly, I have never tried! So, who's talking to Chuck? What glorious thing is happening in the birthline inside his soul? Methinks he doth protest too much. And, by the way, he does know how much I like him!

There are times when our sharing of the gospel message brings immediate fruit. A soul is ripe for harvest, and a response comes quickly. More often, we must patiently wait. We water, we nurture, we tend, we hoe, we fertilize ... and we pray and wait. Our work is not simple or automatic. We need to take a deep breath, allow ourselves to be human, and accept our own faults and failures. We need to feel free to look and laugh at our own hang-ups, to try something different, to step on a landmine or two.

Recently, one of my dear blues buddies looked me in the eyes, and I knew that a dance step was coming — a lead and follow, the question-answer dance. The question came: "Pastor Al, are we just a bunch of lab rats for you?" I thought for a moment before I answered. "Absolutely," I said. "And I am to you, my friend. See if this stuff is working for me, too, that's fair." It was her cautious baby step to test out how real I was, whether my presence and interest were simply a manipulation of my own agenda. Her eyes were still mildly suspicious, but our friendship was intact.

Spiritual conversations

I was sitting in the waiting room of Merchant's Tire & Auto Center. You know, the one with Tires Today magazines for recreational reading, while your car is put through the paces to reveal that everything is broken? I looked up and saw a Buddhist monk, wearing the distinctive orange, wrapped robe and leather sandals and smooth head, walking from his car toward the glass front door of Merchants. The guys behind the counter saw him, too, and one of them said, "Don't look now, but here comes the Dalai Lama." The monk opened the door and went up to the counter. His accent was strong - probably Vietnamese. I pretended to read my "Adventures in Tires" article.

The monk said, "I need new tires," the words a bit difficult to understand through the distinct accent. Bubba looked puzzled, not quite able to make out the request. The monk asked again, his diction no better than the first attempt.

Bubba, missing the obvious request, answered loudly and slowly, "We are not hiring anyone right now." It was killing me. Even though I wanted to sit and watch this comedy, I stepped in to help the conversation. "Our friend needs new tires."

"Well, why didn't he say so?"

I grinned. "We aren't very smart on this side of the counter, you know?" Bubba handed the clipboard to my new friend. We had a great chat as we sat in the waiting room, and a week later he stopped by the church to talk.

Interpreting, I recently understood, is how I have lived my life. Instead of hearing what people say, I seem to be wired to hear what's behind their words. Growing up in a chaotic home, I came to expect that from one second to the next, a cherished family memory could be transformed into a lifelong wound inflicted by harsh, angry words. I needed to develop radar and feelers to know what to expect at any moment. Lots of other people I meet have this orientation, and many don't. Nobody gets the whole package to navigate this bumpy, unpredictable road of life. We must all learn to trust and rely on others' gifts to get us through the confusion.

Listening to the unchurched, I tend to hear the image of God speaking. If all of us are made in the image of God, that image can't stop bubbling out. We all have our guarded moments, when we choose each word perfectly and maintain the exterior we want others to see. We also have unguarded moments, when the soul speaks from somewhere else. When our bodies hurt and physical or emotional pain erupts; when we watch a sunset or attend a funeral; when we go fishing and feel the thrill of the catch; or when we feel the pleasure of molding clay in a pottery class, our souls bubble to the surface. If we listen carefully, we can often discern spiritual conversations in those moments, and the image of God in the unbeliever peeks out. A door of connection can begin to open if we listen to really hear. The possibility of planting a seed of trust exists in that sacred moment.

But are we able to pick up on *spiritual* conversations, or do we only hear *religious* ones? In the church we have a language, a culture, a way of thinking and being that has become a real barrier to hearing what a non-Christian is saying to us. I realized recently that I am an EQ *(emotional intelligence)* guy in an IQ denomination. IQ hears facts and can process great volumes of information, something I have been jealous of my whole life. EQ uses different eyes, ears, and processors. In my Presbyterian denomination, we value doctrine, and systems of doctrine, and systems to systematize our doctrine. I wonder: do we run the risk of becoming so enamored with our doctrinal definitions and distinctions that we miss the amazing connections waiting for us in the people around us? They are all around us...if we would only open our eyes and ears.

Expect divine appointments

Kung Fu was an American action-adventure western drama series starring David Carradine. The series aired on ABC from October 1972 to April 1975, for a total of 63 episodes. *Kung Fu* was based on a simple, unencumbered philosophy of life. You simply walked the earth. That's right: you would encounter the things you are meant to experience, the people you are supposed to meet, and the dangers that will shape what you are meant to be. Kung Fu had one providential experience after another — fighting the bad guys, assisting the desperate, and living in the tension of each appointed encounter.

Could it be that God has designed divine appointments in our weeks and days, and it is up to us to be available to them? Once, when I had finally given up all that terrible fast food from McDonald's, I was sitting in the late night drive-through of Burger King. I waited for a voice from the speaker to ask me for my order. Annoying silence. I imagined that the kids at the workstations were looking at me through the camera and drawing mustaches on the screen. I finally got out of my car and walked up to the window. There stood a middle-aged woman, not a kid, and she was visibly upset. I asked her what was wrong. She said, "My babysitter just called, and my little boy fell down the stairs." I asked her if I could pray for him. "Yes", she said, "his name is Juan." I said a fast-food prayer and got my food, as she asked the next person, "Can I help you?" As I walked back to my car, she gave me a smile of thanks, holding her hand on her heart.

Brothers and sisters, can you imagine a life designed by God where divine appointments that are created in eternity can come about in a fast food drive-thru? Maybe we need to be constantly living in the expectation of what God might be up to today — in and through me — in whatever situations surround me.

Refresh the evangelist

It is not only the unchurched that need us to be present. True, we need to spend time with them and hear their hurts, and much later we can weave their stories into the story of the gospel. To do this effectively, we must let listening give way to hearing. In this same gentle way, we need to be encouraging to the tired, frightened, beaten-down evangelists and regular garden-variety Christians working alongside us. Writing this book is, more than anything else, a way to give new respect and space to the individuals who will lead this new charge. Many capable Christians are sitting at the door of souls coming into heaven, and they too need encouragement.

As a pastor for nearly 25 years, I know the difficulties well. The landmines hidden in our own souls are always ready to explode. So we run to hide behind our doctrine, our pulpits, our church culture, and our intellectualism — our strike-before-being-struck style of talking. I get it. Many of us are in full evangelism retreat, at most inviting one or two acquaintances to Easter service.

So, I honor and appreciate those who took their posts in the past in the world of evangelism. We should love and honor our pastors and missionaries who gave up much, as did their families, to devote their lives to sharing the message that Jesus saves sinners. And I long to carry the torch and pass it along as we move into a new season of evangelism. Dear ones let's refresh our fellow evangelists; let's encourage one another. There is much work to be done, and we are in this labor of love together.

Go to "your" blues bar

I quickly understood that the blues bar folks would come into my home but would never darken the door to my church. Some of them said it was full of hypocrites: "I already know I am one; why join others?" Others were afraid of judgment — "Lightening will strike!" — and others of being overly marketed — "That's a sales booth, and once you enter you can never get out." Some held grudges from deep in the past: "My grandfather said he would never, ever go back even when he died; he insisted his funeral be in a funeral home."

There are all kinds of reasons people avoid the church. Most people in your town or neighborhood will never "get religion" by going to church. If we long to draw the lost, perhaps we need to stop waiting in our church pews, and begin to prayerfully seek out our own "blues bar." Perhaps your blues bar will be a knitting gathering, a sci-fi movie club, a NASCAR race, or a dance. Maybe it's your bowling league, your running club, your VFW hall. We will need to meet them on *their* territory, not ours. Go with an open heart. Go without a script or preconceived expectations. Go expecting to meet fellow image-bearers. Stay curious. Listen to hear. Watch God unfold a divine appointment as you befriend people, laugh with them, and enter into their world.

Amazing discoveries wait for you, my friend, discoveries within your own soul, treasures waiting to be mined. And people ... eternal souls fashioned by the God of the universe ... needing someone who cares enough to listen, to love, to live out the gospel, even in the middle of a blues bar.

Study Guide

Chapter 1 - Listening in a Blues Bar

1. I have shared something of my own story in this first chapter - some of my very real struggles as a pastor and an evangelist. Can you share something from your past that you carry with you, something that helps the other group members know you're a real person and not a "perfect Christian"?

2. If you wrote a blues song, what would be its title and verse?

3. Where might your blues bar be? (bowling league, knitting club, dance class, coffee shop, yoga class, etc.)

4. Who in your life might be trying to tell you their blues story? What stands in the way of hearing them?

5. Have you ever observed or been a part of a group who are deeply bonded to one another, despite the absence of a common faith-connection?

6. Can you take a go at describing or defining the "post-Christian age"?

7. Where does this first chapter leave you? Eager to move ahead? Afraid of what might be around the corner?

Chapter 2 - It's All About Suffering

1. Does your history - like mine - have a "pivotal moment"?

2. How does your pivotal moment shape the way in which you understand and approach the unchurched?

3. What do you think of this statement: As Christians, "we perfect a kind of dualism, a contrast between the life we really live, and the life we present in our 'witnessing monologues'"?

4. Why are we driven by fear of failure?

5. How does our apologetics help? Or hurt?

6. How do you think the thief on the cross came to faith?

7. What do you think of the "front narrative"/ "back narrative" concept?

Chapter 3 - We Are Not Present

1. Can you relate an experience of not "being present"?

2. "What uses up all the space where "being present" needs to be nurtured? Our pain does. Pain can use up all our extra space and push out the opportunity to grow a new relationship. Our minds continue to grind over...."

   What are your thoughts about the above paragraph?

3. What do you fear about evangelism? Be as honest as you can.

4. Do you think we are too much "in our theology"?

5. How can we be salt and light without being condemning?

6. What are your thoughts about evangelism scripts? Have you ever used one, with or without success?

7. What is the biggest obstacle to your being present with a hurting person?

Chapter 4 - Our "Joseph" Story

1. Did God deliberately allow Joseph to be thrown into a pit by his brothers, and then sold into slavery?

2. Has God deliberately allowed pain in your life? To what end?

3. Why is it that many church members will not discuss their difficulties and often pretend that they do not exist?

4. Do we have a "tone problem" when talking with unbelievers? Do we feel a need to seem as though we have our act together?

5. How do we react to fellow Christians who have current or past "messy lives"?

6. Do we allow our pastors the space and grace to be imperfect?

Chapter 5 - The Mother of All Questions

1. Can you remember an instance of hiding (yourself, or something you did) from your parents? Was it a successful attempt?

2. Why do you think God asked Adam "Where are you?", when He certainly knew where he was?

3. "Could it be that, just as God speaks the mother of all questions in the scripture, all humans carry this question around in their souls? Could it be that the soul wrestles, ponders, imagines, and hopes far more than is evident on the surface, as each of us asks, 'Where am I?' " What do you think of this quote?

4. Do believers do their hiding within the walls of the church?

5. In your interactions with unbelievers, do you sense the image of God in them, or is it hard to see?

6. How can we be more attuned to perceiving the image of God in those around us?

Chapter 6 - The Birth Line

This chapter is an introspective - and very personal - one. Take some time with your study group to reflect on your own spiritual birthline, and how both subtle and obvious influences have shaped your unique journey in faith.

Chapter 7 - The Image of God is Speaking

1. Do you think the image of God is evident in the unbeliever? If it is, how and where do you detect it?

2. How has sin affected that image, both in the believer and the unbeliever? Is there a difference?

3. Respond to the following quote: "They pick up on our dualism: happy, happy in public, but sad and tormented in secret.... Yes, God harnesses even the blackness of death to bring about Life. And I think the non-churched want to be welcomed into our suffering."

4. Do you think the idea of the Judeo-Christian ethic, which underlies Western society, is a good starting place for evangelism?

5. Why is the Judeo-Christian ethic a foreign concept to most people?

6. Why are non-Christians cynical about the established church, even those that try to be "seeker-friendly"?

7. What do you think of "The Five Questions"? What are your thoughts about asking them and listening to the answers without offering any response of your own?

Chapter 8 - The Resurrection of Sabbath

1. How do you like to keep the Sabbath?

2. Why do you think God commanded His people to keep the Sabbath?

3. Respond to this quote by C.S. Lewis: "We live, in fact, in a world starved for solitude, silence, and private: and therefore starved for meditation and true friendship."

4. What current cultural forces gravitate against Sabbath rest?

5. Is keeping the Sabbath an art form or a set of rules?

6. Is Sabbath rest best cultivated alone, or with others?

7. How do you wish you could better keep the spirit of the Sabbath?

Chapter 9 - Where Do We Go from Here?

1. "As we listen to someone else talking - especially someone with whom we might potentially disagree - we are always framing a response....a 'yeah, but!' That 'yeah, but' steals our hearing." Does this sound familiar to you?

2. How likely are you to see or hear the image of God in people who are very different from you?

3. Why are we afraid of people who are different from us?

4. Have you had any divine appointments recently? If so, would you share this with your group?

5. Do you feel the need for refreshment from fellow believers?

6. Where is your blues bar? Can you think of one person you could pray to connect with there?

7. Where do *you* want to go from here?

Acknowledgements

I thank, first of all, my ever-serving, unstoppable, art-passionate wife, who loves me and wakes to see if I'm sleeping okay. You have a phrase that changes me: "Can I help you?" And you do. Your advice, editing, patience, and endless acts of service astound me. Our love adventure is 37 years old and growing, and I'm ready for the highs and lows to come, as long as we do it together. I love you, Deb.

I thank my mentoring children, Erin and Wesley, who love being alive, laugh at my jokes, and teach me who Jesus is. (Oh, the fun still to come!)

I owe great thanks to my parents, Al and Hope Dayhoff: Mom, you were the first blues singer in my life, and Dad, you said it would all be better in the morning. I'm just now beginning to get it.

To Chris Labs and Harry Watt, our ET board members, who mentor me with sage advice, Olympic-size self- deprecating humor, and deep life friendship. Let's fish, smoke cigars, and repeat.

To Lauren Bleam, who took a very active and effective role in shaping this book and welcomed in others. And to the faithful readers who gave her their insights and valuable feedback on each chapter.

To my dear blues buddies (way too many to list!) who have loved me, fed and wined me at their table told me preacher jokes I could either choke on or laugh at. Thank you for allowing me to sit with you, dance with you, and receive healing hugs from you. Let's do this forever! Do I think there's another side called heaven? I do. Let's all make it there, OK? Nobody gets left behind. We make sure, OK?

To Robbin Kapsallis. Your songs, kind friendship and soul in your music always move me to deeper places inside my own soul.

To Brian Hamilton, Pastor of Westminster Presbyterian Church in Washington DC. You have taught me to look for the unseen person. You introduced me to the subtle complexities of racism, poverty, and a church of humans like me seeking their way in this crazy world. Your flock has loved me and I have felt its realness. When I asked the group of elderly ladies with hats "Can I join your club," you all said, "You're already in!" Please never end Blue Monday — it's part of my life.

To Clare Wolfowitz: you are a gift my friend. You are the master of "dance like no one is watching." Your patience with me as you edit, adapting to fit into my thoughts, intents and trajectory, makes me let down my guard. I can see new colors, hear new music, and delight in blues lyrics that hit bone deep.

Many thanks to Connie Van Til for a labor of passion and love. Your patience, steadiness in storms, and use of your gifts made this second edition possible.

To the blues musicians, some who are listed in this book and some I know only as the drummer or bass player at a blues jam. You are playing God's music, describing the weight of a cursed and a vice-gripped world that can be oh-so-cruel. I strangely feel encouragement from your sound and the lyrics that speak it as it is.

To Blue Church: let's grow from inside the bar and reach outward. We can still be a church that meets in a blues bar — and also a blues bar that meets for church. New followers of Jesus have that "new car smell" that makes me smile and give me hope.

About the Author

Rev. Allan Dayhoff is the Founder and Executive Director of Evangelize Today, an evangelical outreach organization that offers a pioneering one- to three-day seminar, designed to give participants the opportunity to reflect on their own conversion process and to apply those insights. More information can be found at www.evangelizetoday.info.

He also serves as Senior Pastor of Grace Fellowship Church, which he founded in 1992. He previously headed Dayhoff Construction.

Rev. Dayhoff earned a Doctor of Ministries at Covenant Theological Seminary in St. Louis, MO. He wrote his dissertation on "Confrontational Monologue vs. Relational Dialogue, as it Relates to the Image of God in the Non- Christian and the Transfer of Faith."

What people in the Blues Bar are saying...

My girlfriend and I were driving west on route fifty on a hot Sunday afternoon and planning to stop at JV's, an ancient biker bar and live music joint.

We had barely taken our seats at the bar and ordered a couple longnecks, when someone announced that the lesson in "blues dancing" was about to begin. Blues dancing? Dance lessons? Jeni and I exchanged glances and I asked if anyone could join in...

Afterwards, we said our thank yous, put some money in the bucket, returned to our seats at the bar as the others sat down together across the room. Someone introducing himself as Bill asked if we wanted to join them for church service. *Church service?* In a biker bar? Why not? So we took our beers with us as we joined the others...

I have never been a churchgoer. Both my parents were raised in religious homes before becoming lifelong atheists in their early twenties. Dad in particular had grown up with a deep antipathy for organized religion...Yet strangely, my curiosity about Jesus and his teachings didn't go away as I grew up...

Jeni and I have been attending all summer. It's the longest I have ever attended church anywhere. Reverend Al and his lovely wife Deb have been a great comfort to Jeni, which makes them a comfort to me...

Chris

I have been fascinated with Pastor Al's radical approach: his return to Jesus' early practice of going amongst the people, especially those broken.

Linda

Pastor Al is a true demonstration of passion, leadership and practicing what he preaches...He's a blessing to everyone that may cross his path...

Jenn the bartender

Pastor Al is a breath of fresh air in the spiritual world. He has a unique style of spreading God's word. In my view, he is not only a pastor, but I consider him a wise friend with a special gift.

Ken

Reverend Al has brought his intense love for God and his passion for people and placed it squarely in the middle of a Blues Bar. Having been scared off from organized religion, I would never have entered a church. Al doesn't push or prod nor guilt or gloat about his faith; rather, he takes your hand and looks you in the eye….I've never felt more heard and understood and less afraid to approach God in prayer and spirit.

Jan

Pastor Al is an open-hearted person who is there for everyone. Blue Church is a totally radical concept. But it works. It touches real people in a real way. My spiritual journey has led me to Blue Church.

Aldo

Pastor Al is a true inspiration. He always wants to know how you are (and he really wants to know), he's ready to offer sound advice, or just be there to listen. People come into your life from time to time for various reasons. I don't even care why he is in my life. I am just glad he is; I am much better off with people like Pastor Al around.

Josh Allen
(lead: Josh Allen Band)

Praise for *Church in a Blues* Bar and *Evangelize Today*

Apologetics, the ability to "give a word back," begins not with talking but with listening to hear — that is, treating my fellow *Imago Dei* (image of God) bearer with dignity and respect. "Giving a word back" begins with realizing that life for many for our fellow *Imago Dei* bearers is not a life of "living happily ever after"; rather, life has dealt many of our neighbors an awfully "bad hand." So, this book asks (and answers) the question, "How do I show respect and dignity to my fellow imago bearer?" Answer: "Tarry long in listening — with your hand over your mouth."

Dr. Luke Bobo, BBT Curriculum Director & Resident Theologian; a former Director of the Francis Schaeffer Institute, Covenant Theological Seminary, St. Louis, MO

The core gospel is always there. What Al does, like a skilled travel guide, is to take us on a journey of re- discovery of too-familiar territory. What we hear as "new" is actually quite old, so old we forgot we knew it: that God not only loves the people he has made, he sort of likes them. And then God invites us to join Him in his affection for people — and to follow the path of affection into respectful listening and truth telling. Al, like the Holy Spirit, catalyzes affection and respect for people. Al's seminar is a special gift.

Rev. Tory K. Baucum, Rector Truro Anglican Church

I wanted you all to know about a new ministry called Evangelize Today that I am very excited about. . . . I went through one of these workshops and it revolutionized my understanding of evangelism and gave me some great tools for becoming more consistent in my own life.

Rev. Tom Herrick, Executive Director Titus Church Planting

I recently attended a daylong Evangelize Today seminar, hosted and facilitated by Rev. Al Dayhoff. The first step in that process was an introspective look at my own life, from before I was born to the present — the good, the bad, and the ugly! Then, Al had me focus on my Christian walk, which did not start with the moment I first believed — it started when I was born, or even before I was born. Finally, Al showed us a way we could gently engage with someone on our heart, in a conversation about God that is not threatening in any way and produces some pretty amazing results! I found going through this process to be extremely edifying, opening doors to better evangelize to those I love, with a beautiful result which brought tears to my eyes. I most strongly recommend Al's training to any church interested in equipping and energizing its congregation!

Bob Tate, Executive Director Truro Anglican Church

Over the course of over 40 years in full-time ministry, I have been through countless evangelism seminars and led a few on my own; but none like Evangelize Today. ET stimulated my curiosity about others, to recognize our common human condition (suffering in a fallen world) and to see how that can be a bridge that ties our lives together and opens wide the door for Jesus to enter. This approach is especially appropriate to our postmodern world. I'd highly recommend it to anyone!

Larry Hoop
Original Vision Network
Coordinator of the PCA Original Vision Ministries

We were looking for something that would really develop the average believer in Jesus Christ to be able to share their faith and have conversations that would develop within their network of friendships. . . The Evangelize Today Seminar really fits that particular model very, very, well.

Dr. Herb Ruby
Senior Pastor, Covenant of Grace Church

Stepping outside our pain in order to make room for others: [the book] really connected [with my congregation]. People, I suspect, saw evangelism for the first time as not a burden but an opportunity . . . you are offering a perspective that might actually set some folks free to love, free to say, "tell me more."

Dr. David B. Wallover, Senior Pastor
Harvest Presbyterian Church, Medina, OH